I0434887

TABLE OF CONTENTS

i

ACRONYMS

2 PPCLI	2nd Battalion, Princess Patricia's Canadian Light Infantry
ANZUS	Australia, New Zealand, United States Security Treaty
DPRK	Democratic People's Republic of Korea
EUSA	Eighth United States Army
JCS	Joint Chiefs of Staff
JP	Joint Publication
NATO	North Atlantic Treaty Organization
OEF	Operation Enduring Freedom
OIF	Operation Iraqi Freedom
POW	Prisoners of War
PRC	People's Republic of China
ROK	Republic of Korea
UN	United Nations

CHAPTER 1

INTRODUCTION

Joint Publication 3-16

But listening for the trumpet, they had received instead orders to Korea, telling them to go and serve, not saying why.

— T.R. Fehrenbach, *This Kind of War*

Joint Publication (JP) 3-16, *Multinational Operations* provides to the joint forces of the United States military a doctrinal foundation for the conduct of coalition warfare. JP 3-16 originated with the consideration that "no one nation–no matter how powerful–can meet global challenges alone."[1] Future American military operations, regardless of their nature, are therefore likely to operate within a coalition framework. This probability is due to considerations such as limited American military resources or the need to demonstrate legitimacy for an operation through international participation. The 1950-1953 Korean War provided American leaders with their first opportunity, absent doctrine, to develop and lead a coalition after the United States assumed status as a "superpower."[2] America subsequently developed and led several coalitions. This poses the question: to what extent does JP 3-16 reflect American experience in building and leading a coalition in Korea in 1950?

---

[1]The President, *National Security Strategy* (Washington, DC: The White House, 2010), http://www.whitehouse.gov/sites/default/files/rss_viewer/national_security_strategy.pdf (accessed August 14, 2013), 1.

[2]Lawrence Freedman, "Introduction," in *British Foreign Policy, 1945-65*, ed. Michael Dockrill and John W. Young (New York: St. Martin's Press, 1989), 2.

The Korean War had three characteristics that merit its use in a study of American doctrine for coalition operations. First, conflict in Korea created a war that President Harry Truman's administration assumed would occur elsewhere, such as Europe. This fact is significant because current instability in the world can prompt unforeseen military actions in unanticipated areas. Second, the militaries from the various contributing nations were not necessarily familiar with each other's operational practices and tactics. Specifically, pre-war military maneuvers did not involve all coalition participants. This fact is critical because coalitions are not always composed of allied nations. Furthermore, future coalition operations are likely to require a rapid military presence regardless of unfamiliarity between coalition partners. Finally, the coalition made war in Korea by employing limited means to achieve limited ends. This factor is significant because future coalition operations, heavily dependent on political will, are unlikely to employ unlimited means or seek unlimited ends.

The United States participated in several coalitions prior to Korea. It sought and received French military assistance through an alliance during the American War for Independence. The United States joined the Anglo-French alliance during the First World War. Subsequently, the United States allied itself principally with Britain and the Soviet Union during World War II. In these examples, the United States was not a global superpower. Therefore, American leaders were not in positions of political or military dominance sufficient to make and enforce independent decisions. Additionally, these examples reflect partnerships that originated after their respective wars began.

The United States did not gain French assistance for the War for Independence until its army demonstrated enough battlefield competence to assure France that victory against Great Britain was possible. American government and military leaders then spent much of the remainder of the war disagreeing with the French on strategy. The United States did not enter World War I until three years after it began. Furthermore, the United States served as an associate power, rather than as an ally to France and Britain, and thus was a junior member of the coalition during the First World War.

The 1941-1945 war against Japan is not included in this study for three reasons. First, as in World War I, the United States did not immediately participate at the beginning of combat operations in the Pacific theater during World War II. Second, World War II's Pacific theater grew into "an American show"[3] after the United States declared war on Japan. American leaders, thus, did not attach significance to operations that did not include American forces.

Third, Soviet participation in the war against Japan was not immediately available. The Soviet Union declared war on Japan on August 8, 1945. Japan agreed to American surrender terms on August 14, 1945.[4] Therefore, the Soviet Union participated in the war against Japan for approximately six days. The United States, thus, independently planned and conducted the majority of Pacific operations without a partner of equal status after declaring war on Japan. America's situation was different in the Second World War's European and the Mediterranean theaters.

---

[3]M. L. Dockrill, "The Foreign Office, Anglo-American Relations and the Korean War, June 1950-June 1951," *International Affairs (Royal Institute of International Affairs 1944)* 62, no. 3 (Summer 1986): 459.

[4]Rufus E. Miles Jr., "Hiroshima: The Strange Myth of Half a Million American Lives Saved," *International Security* 10, no. 2 (Autumn 1985): 129.

America's partnership with Great Britain during World War II, specifically in the Mediterranean and European theaters of war, represents the closest example to America's coalition leadership position in Korea. The United States entered World War II in the European and Mediterranean theaters as Britain's junior partner in men, materiél, and combat experience. The United States quickly dominated its partner in war materiél production and supplied the majority of Allied personnel to Western Europe by January 1944.[5] Contribution levels aside, Anglo-American operations in the Mediterranean and European theaters occurred within an "integrated command structure." In this arrangement, one member nation provides the strategic commander while the deputy commanders and staff are soldiers from contributing nations.[6]

The United States and Great Britain shared responsibility for military operations in the Mediterranean and European theaters. This example's similarities to Korea are related to America's growing dominance in men and materiél. American leaders assumed a more authoritative leadership role as their nation's contributions increased during the course of the Second World War. However, they still had to achieve common understanding and objectives with their British partners to sustain the coalition. Leaders such as President Franklin Roosevelt and General Dwight D. Eisenhower ensured that American personnel acted in a manner that sustained the Anglo-American coalition. The Anglo-American coalition, along with the Soviet Union, defeated their enemy. Thus, in

---

[5]M. A. Fitzsimmons, *The Foreign Policy of the British Labour Government 1945-1951* (Notre Dame, IN: University of Notre Dame Press, 1953), 19.

[6]Chairman, Joint Chiefs of Staff, Joint Publication 3-16, *Multinational Operations* (Washington, DC: Government Printing Office, 2007), xii.

coalition warfare, the art of sustaining the coalition is as significant as the conduct of military operations.

Several factors reduced the United States' ability to lead the coalitions in which it served prior to the Korean War. During the American War for Independence, for example, the French were not immediate partners and subsequently attempted to assert themselves as coalition leaders. The United States did not possess primary responsibility for the conduct of operations during the First World War because it joined the coalition too late to earn a voice of leadership. Similarly, American-Soviet operations in the Pacific did not last long enough to call them coalition operations. Likewise, the Anglo-American coalition in the European and Mediterranean theaters shared responsibility for operations. It is for these reasons that America's leadership in Korea, dominant and undeniable throughout the entire war, is relevant to this study.

The coalition in Korea followed a "lead nation command structure." Under this structure, contributing nations place their military forces under the command and control of one nation.[7] That America, as the world's noncommunist superpower, would lead the coalition in Korea was undisputed. The United States, in contrast to its previous coalition experiences, not only entered the war with, but retained primary responsibility for decision-making, and thus, for the coalition's conduct of the war. Compromising with partners, a critical component of JP 3-16, became critical to sustaining the coalition in Korea. Specifically, United States leaders needed to avoid abusing their dominant leadership position in Korea to sustain their coalition.

---

[7]Ibid., xii.

Joint Publication 3-16's doctrine is not directive in nature. Its guidance is not definitive or uncompromising. However, the publication exists as the current joint American guide for coalition operations. Therefore, utilizing its guidance is necessary to the development of this study. JP 3-16 defines coalition operations as military actions conducted by the armed forces of two or more nations.[8] Coalitions, thus, are multinational in composition. Coalition partners are potentially already members of an existing alliance, a structure typically permanent in nature. Non-allied nations can also contribute military forces to coalitions. A coalition, thus, is an organization created by "*ad hoc* agreement . . . for common action."[9] Such an organization, composed of members of the United Nations (UN), served under American leadership in the Korean War.

The 1950-1953 Korean War reflects a coalition formed on an *ad hoc* basis for common action. Of the 16 nations contributing forces to Korea, the most relevant to this study include the United States, Great Britain, Canada, and Australia. American relationships with other members of the "English-speaking world"[10] before the Korean War are significant areas of focus in this study. Great Britain, Canada, and Australia were critical American partners during and after the Second World War. Great Britain shared a "special relationship"[11] with the United States. Canada and Australia shared common

---

[8]Ibid., I-1.

[9]Ibid.

[10]Winston S. Churchill, *Blood, Sweat, and Tears* (New York: G. P. Putnam's Sons, 1941), 447.

[11]Gordon A. Craig, "The Political Leader as Strategist," in *Makers of Modern Strategy*, ed. Peter Paret (New Jersey: Princeton University Press, 1986), 501.

histories with the United States as former British colonies. Furthermore, Canada's proximity to the United States and Australia's efforts to improve its diplomatic and military relations with the United States after 1945 merit these nations' inclusion in this study.

JP 3-16 promotes four tenets for the conduct of coalition operations.[12] They are respect, rapport, knowledge of partners, and patience. Respect advises American forces to acknowledge that a partner's national prestige and honor are "as important . . . as combat capability"[13] and the size of its contribution. Therefore, American political and military should respect multinational contributions regardless of size. Additionally, partners should be included in planning and decision-making regardless of contribution size or type. Including partners in these deliberations helps build the second tenet. Rapport recommends that leaders at all levels develop teamwork to achieve unity of effort with partners of various nationalities. Unity of effort means that all partners work together to achieve the same objective. Achieving unity of effort, therefore, is critical to sustaining a coalition until its mission is complete.

Knowledge of partners is JP 3-16's third tenet. It encourages American military leaders to dedicate similar if not more time and effort to understand their coalition partners' perspectives and histories as they do to understanding the enemy's capabilities and tactics. This effort demonstrates appreciation for partner contributions and, thus, enhances unity of effort. Patience is JP 3-16's fourth tenet. It is included to remind coalition leaders of their responsibility to understand considerations such as the reasons

---

[12]Chairman, Joint Chiefs of Staff, Joint Publication 3-16 (2007), I-3 – I-4.

[13]Ibid., ix.

behind the restrictions a contributing nation may place on the employment of their forces. This tenet requires a significant investment of time to develop trust and cohesion with coalition partners.

In addition to the four tenets, JP 3-16 provides additional guidance for coalition development and leadership. First, it states that political considerations typically motivate a nation's decision to contribute military forces to a coalition.[14] States may decide to join an American led coalition for the mere purpose of showing their flag alongside that of the United States. Therefore, nations typically contribute forces to coalitions to support long-term national objectives. In American led coalitions, these objectives are likely to include stronger relations with the United States upon completion of the coalition's mission.

This guidance aligns with the tenet of respect for national prestige. Nicaragua, for example, was the second member of the UN to announce its intention to provide ground forces to Korea.[15] International expectations for Nicaragua to contribute substantial combat forces were minimal. However, Nicaragua's announcement demonstrated its solidarity with the world's noncommunist superpower. Therefore, American leaders had to respect its offer regardless of the reason behind it.

Joint Publication 3-16 also cautions against expecting automatic contributions from current allies. Its warning is relevant to the American military. JP 3-16 identifies the possibility that financial or political restrictions may prevent allies from contributing to an *ad hoc* force. For example, Great Britain was an American ally in June 1950. Britain

---

[14]Ibid., I-1.

[15]U.S. Department of State, World Reaction to Korean Developments, No. 22, July 19, 1950, Harry S. Truman Library, Independence, MO.

had yet to offer specific contributions to Korea when Nicaragua announced its intentions on July 19, 1950. The deployment of substantial British military forces to areas such as Malaya and Greece caused this delay.[16] Therefore, American leaders should have recognized Britain's limitations and thereby avoid expectations of automatic British contributions.

Coalition leaders, therefore, must respect the fact that political objectives motivate a state's decision to contribute or withhold forces from the coalition. Furthermore, political considerations are also likely to affect the timing behind a nation's contribution of forces. For example, Australia's government announced that it would contribute forces to Korea one hour before the British government announced similar intentions.[17] The Australian government rushed its announcement to beat the British and demonstrate Australia's reliability to the Truman administration. Australia's haste supported its political goals.

Joint Publication 3-16's guidance additionally emphasizes building "mutual confidence"[18] between contributing nations to ensure coalition success. Mutual confidence represents a critical requirement to building unity of effort between coalition members. General of the Army Dwight D. Eisenhower highlighted mutual confidence as a concept basic in nature but critical to a coalition's ability to accomplish its mission.[19]

---

[16]U.S. Department of State, Message from Mr. Attlee to the President, July 6, 1950, Harry S. Truman Library, Independence, MO.

[17]Jeffrey Grey, *The Commonwealth Armies and the Korean War* (Manchester, UK: Manchester University Press, 1988), 35.

[18]Chairman, Joint Chiefs of Staff, Joint Publication 3-16 (2007), I-3.

[19]Ibid., I-3.

For example, contributors to a coalition operating in a "lead nation" command structure should have confidence in the lead nation's resolve to accomplish the coalition mission. Additionally, military personnel should have confidence in their partners' ability to contribute militarily to the coalition's mission. Coalition operations are unlikely to achieve success if contributing members cannot achieve unity of effort through mutual confidence.

Joint Publication 3-16 additionally recommends that the coalition commander account for capability differences between contributing nations. This concept parallels the tenet of knowing one's partners. National laws, military doctrine and weapons, culture, religion, language, and political structures and ideologies are not necessarily military capabilities. However, they are but a few of the differences likely to exist between coalition partners. Significantly, they influence the means a nation's military force pursues to make war. Coalition leaders, political or military, are thus obliged to account for those differences in their planning and decision-making.

American coalition doctrine also warns coalition leaders to recognize their limitations regarding areas such as command authority and operational employment. Related to the tenet of patience, leaders must respect and consider matters such as their partners' national caveats. For example, an individual's position as a coalition commander does not necessarily mean that they retain command authority over multinational troops in areas such as discipline. Additionally, contributing nations are likely to restrict their forces to specific operations. Nations apply these stipulations to support their respective policies or goals. Therefore, a coalition commander must ensure that all multinational forces exhibit sufficient respect and understanding for these multinational partner objectives.

JP 3-16 additionally provides two checklist-style principles to ensure reasonable interoperability at political and strategic levels to enhance the coalition's ability to accomplish its mission. First, JP 3-16 emphasizes the lead nation's responsibility to develop strategic guidance to the commander in conjunction with coalition partners.[20] Strategic guidance includes defining clear political objectives and identifying likely military tasks. Outlining goals and tasks is significant. Operations with clear and achievable objectives are likely to receive multinational contributions. Conversely, operations with objectives perceived as unclear or unattainable are unlikely to receive coalition contributions. Furthermore, changing strategic guidance while an operation is ongoing increases confusion, reduces unity of effort, and dissuades states from keeping their military forces in the coalition.

The second principle found in JP 3-16 is its recommendation for the lead nation to define the coalition's exit strategy and its desired military end state.[21] These criteria are significant because they allow coalition partners to define military success to their domestic constituency. This opportunity thus increases a nation's potential to contribute combat forces. Additionally, these criteria help reduce possibilities for domestic friction or dissatisfaction with United States policy to arise within a contributing nation over the course of an operation.

---

[20]Ibid., A-1.

[21]Ibid., A-3.

11

Guidance, principles, and tenets from JP 3-16 share many similarities with the Korean War. For example, UN forces crossed the 38th Parallel after achieving their initial objective by restoring stability in South Korea. The decision to move north of the 38th Parallel escalated the conflict by bringing China into the war. China's invasion created a stalemate and, thus, prolonged the war. These events created conditions that challenged the responsibility of American leaders to sustain mutual confidence and unity of effort with their Commonwealth partners.

Background to the Korean War

The United States, the Soviet Union, and Great Britain agreed to divide the Korean peninsula at the 38th Parallel following the conclusion of World War II. These nations created the line as a temporary measure to begin "liquidating Japanese rule"[22] from the Korean peninsula. The Soviet Union assumed administrative responsibility for Korea north of the 38th Parallel, while the United States assumed administrative responsibility for the nation south of that line. The Soviet Union and the United States thus administered the surrender, processing, and return of Japanese troops to Japan within their respective Korean zones of occupation. President Harry Truman's administration identified Korea as a "peripheral concern"[23] to strategically important areas such as Western Europe and Japan.

---

[22]Dean Acheson, *The Korean War* (New York: W.W. Norton & Company, 1971), 1.

[23]John Lewis Gaddis, *We Now Know: Rethinking Cold War History* (New York: Oxford University Press, 1997), 58.

The Truman administration's perspective on Korea's importance prior to 1950 is remarkable for three reasons. First, the Soviet Union maintained troops on the peninsula until 1948. This fact infers potential for a Soviet attack against Japan, a possibility Stalin considered likely "if the Americans continue their current policy"[24] of Japanese economic development. Second, Korea is close in proximity to Japan. Therefore, a continuation of current American policy could induce Stalin to preemptively attack Japan and secure the Soviet Union's eastern border.

American perspectives on Korea are also remarkable because of America's growing antagonism with the Soviet Union. Disagreements on the occupation of Germany after 1945 helped to create the American—Soviet departure from a wartime alliance. Truman's administration disagreed severely with the Soviets over the management of Korean affairs and Korea's post-occupation future immediately after stationing American troops on the peninsula. Specifically, American and Soviet leaders wanted Korea to adopt their respective ideologies. If Korea truly presented a peripheral concern to American security, Truman's administration should have removed American forces from the peninsula immediately after liquidating Japan's forces. However, the Truman administration did not do this.

Soviet aggression in Europe prevented Truman's administration from immediately removing American forces from Korea. The Soviet blockade of Berlin in 1948 reflected Soviet intentions to use military force to achieve a favorable political solution.[25] Overt evidence did not exist in the late 1940s to prove that the Soviets would

---

[24]Ibid., 72.

[25]Ibid.

not use their occupation zone in Korea as a staging location to attack Japan's "economic, social, and political unrest."[26] Thus, it is conceivable with hindsight to conclude that Soviet aggression was likely to remain not isolated to Europe.

The Soviet Union did not invade Japan after 1945. However, American efforts to rebuild Japan worried Stalin. The Soviets, sharing a border with Korea, did not need to maintain permanently troops on the peninsula if Stalin chose to invade Japan. They could simply rely on the presence of a friendly communist government in northern Korea to position troops prior to an assault. It is likely that Truman's preoccupation with Europe prevented him from recognizing this possibility. Regardless, United States troops continued to occupy the America's zone in Korea until 1948. Given these considerations, it appears that American leaders were wrong to identify Korea as "strategically unimportant"[27] to United States security.

Dean Acheson, Truman's Secretary of State, recommended that a simultaneous American-Soviet withdrawal from Korea occur in conjunction with UN sponsored Korean elections in 1948.[28] Acheson's recommendation supported Truman's domestic and international goals. Domestically, reducing the American military presence and elections in Korea allowed Truman to demonstrate increasing global stability to the American public.

---

[26]Thomas E. Hanson, *Combat Ready? The Eighth U.S. Army on the Eve of the Korean War* (College Station: Texas A&M University Press, 2010), 16.

[27]D. Clayton James with Anne Sharpe Wells, *Refighting the Last War: Command and Crisis in Korea 1950-1953* (New York: The Free Press, 1993), 2.

[28]Acheson, *The Korean War*, 2.

Internationally, Acheson's recommendation benefitted the United States in three ways. First, a self-reliant Korea allowed the Truman administration to withdraw American troops from the peninsula without creating an international perception that the United States was retreating ideologically from the Soviet threat.[29] Second, successful elections would depict Korea as a nation capable of self-government without reliance on foreign assistance. Thus, successful Korean elections, rather than an outright American withdrawal, presented the smallest possible risk to American prestige.[30] Finally, successful elections supposedly would also remove Soviet forces and influence from Korea.

The Soviet Union accepted a mutual withdrawal from Korea, but opposed UN sponsored elections.[31] Stalin argued that elections under UN supervision were not necessary because Koreans could achieve independence through the withdrawal of foreign forces and creating Korean solutions to Korean problems.[32] Stalin likely knew that the Koreans, given their ideological divisions, were unlikely to achieve a Korean solution for a unified government. However, a divided Korea left a friendly communist

---

[29]Harry S. Truman, *Memoirs by Harry S. Truman, Volume II: Years of Trial and Hope* (Garden City, NY: Doubleday & Company, 1956), 326.

[30]U.S. Department of State, *Foreign Affairs of the United States 1948, General; The United Nations*, vol. 1, Part Two (Washington, DC: United States Government Printing Office, 1976), 536.

[31]Acheson, *The Korean War*, 2.

[32]Peter Lowe, *The Origins of the Korea War* (New York: Longman, 1986), 42.

government on Stalin's border and, thus, ensured that potential aggressors could not invade the Soviet Union through Korea.[33]

Stalin's willingness to withdraw from Korea, and opposition to supervised elections, demonstrated three considerations. First, Stalin knew his nation had to rebuild itself after World War II. The Soviet Union was, thus, unable to conduct major combat operations immediately after the war. Second, Stalin, concerned about Soviet security, did not want to risk the election of a noncommunist government on his border. He likely understood that the American zone, containing nearly two-thirds of the Korean population,[34] would elect a noncommunist government under UN supervision for all of Korea by virtue of its majority. Third, he wanted to maintain influence in areas wherever possible for future exploitation. Retaining a communist government in northern Korea allowed Stalin to build a strong military force along his border and prevent the West from using the peninsula to act aggressively against the Soviet Union.

Truman's administration recognized that the United States could not give an "unlimited guarantee"[35] to Korean stability. It ignored Soviet objections and secured UN sponsorship for Korean elections. The American occupation zone elected Rhee Syngman and named itself the Republic of Korea (ROK). The Soviet zone did not participate in the UN elections. It selected Kim Il-sung to lead the Democratic People's Republic of Korea

---

[33]Bruce Cumings, *The Origins of the Korean War. Liberation and the Emergence of Separate Regimes 1945-1947* (Princeton: Princeton University Press, 1981), 121.

[34]U.S. Department of State, *Foreign Relations of the United States, 1948: The Far East and Australia*, vol. 6 (Washington, DC: United States Government Printing Office, 1974), 1124.

[35]Lowe, *The Origins of the Korea War*, 47.

(DPRK).[36] The demarcation line at the 38th Parallel, created for temporary means, became permanent unless Rhee or Kim could unify Korea "on their respective terms."[37]

"New responsibilities"[38] helped to accelerate the withdrawal of American combat forces from Korea. Two conditions created the United States' new responsibilities. First, its leaders identified the Soviet Union as a significant threat to global stability. Second, the United States was the only nation to emerge from World War II "stronger and richer at war's end."[39] Therefore, it was the nation most capable of deterring Soviet aggression. From a security perspective, Truman's administration decided that rehabilitating Western Europe's military and financial crises provided the best means to prevent Soviet aggression.[40] However, Truman's administration quickly found its security options limited by domestic considerations.

America's tradition of rapid military demobilization following wars occurred with perhaps more intensity after World War II than any post-war period in American history. Truman, after leaving office, claimed that the American public wanted to "scuttle their military might."[41] American demobilization after World War II reduced the army from

---

[36]Matthew B. Ridgway, *The Korean War* (Garden City, NY: Doubleday & Company, 1967), 8.

[37]Gaddis, *We Now Know: Rethinking Cold War History*, 71.

[38]Freedman, "Introduction," 3.

[39]George C. Herring, *From Colony to Superpower: U.S. Foreign Relations since 1776* (New York: Oxford University Press, 2008), 597.

[40]U.S. Department of State, *Foreign Affairs of the United States 1948*, vol. 1, Part Two, 549.

[41]Truman, *Memoirs by Harry S. Truman, Volume II: Years of Trial and Hope*, 345.

8.5 million personnel in 1945 to 591,487 on June 26, 1950.[42] Clearly, demobilizing the United States Army reduced the Truman administration's ability to meet American security commitments.

Neither Truman nor the American public effectively considered the reality of their nation's new role in global affairs after the Second World War. The United States barely maintained adequate conventional strength to defend its territory. Its atomic bomb monopoly was not sufficient to deter the Soviet's blockade against Berlin. Therefore, it is reasonable to conclude that the American nuclear monopoly would not suffice to deter aggressive Soviet actions elsewhere, particularly after the Soviets detonated an atomic bomb in 1949.[43] Additionally, America's rapid demobilization frightened allies that relied on United States protection.[44] Therefore, America's initial retreat to isolation after World War II encouraged instability in a global environment already swarming with uncertainty.

Instability in Greece and Turkey, regions of British influence prior to World War II, "decisively shattered"[45] the Truman administration's illusions of America's isolation from world affairs. Britain's inability to maintain sufficient "influence and power"[46] to

_____

[42]Hanson, *Combat Ready? The Eighth U.S. Army on the Eve of the Korean War*, 13.

[43]Clay Blair, *The Forgotten War: America in Korea 1950-1953* (New York: Anchor Press, 1989), 20.

[44]Freedman, "Introduction," 3.

[45]Edward A. Koldziej, *The Uncommon Defense and Congress, 1945-1963* (Columbus: Ohio State University Press, 1966), 19.

[46]Michael Dockrill, *British Defence since 1945* (Oxford, UK: Basil Blackwell, 1988), 31.

meet its traditional responsibilities forced Truman to acknowledge the United States'

post-1945 responsibilities to the world. Truman's acknowledgement led to three critical

decisions. First, he created the Truman Doctrine. Second, he initiated steps to begin

rearming the United States military. Third, Truman's administration developed National

Security Council Document 68 (NSC-68).

Truman announced the Truman Doctrine in 1947 to refocus the nation to its

worldwide commitments. His administration reversed its initial post-World War II belief

that attempting to be militarily strong "everywhere runs the risk of being weak

everywhere."[47] The Truman Doctrine, inspired by Truman's decision to support Greece

and Turkey, denied American diplomatic recognition for "any government imposed upon

any nation by the force of any foreign power."[48] Additionally, Truman's doctrine

committed the United States to supporting democratic movements throughout the world.

Furthermore, Truman called for a "modest" military rearmament program in 1948.[49] His

hope for modest rearmament did not hide the fact that he appeared to have recognized his

military's inability to meet America's new commitment.

National Security Council Document 68 was significant to America's foreign and

domestic policy for four reasons. First, it turned "traditional U.S. foreign policy

---

[47]U.S. Department of State, *Foreign Affairs of the United States 1948,* vol. 1, Part Two, 547.

[48]Frank Tannenbaum, "The American Tradition in Foreign Relations," *Foreign Affairs* 30, no. 1 (October 1951): 49.

[49]Walter Millis, "Military Problems of the New Administration," *Foreign Affairs* 31, no. 1 (January 1953): 217.

assumptions upside down"[50] by reversing the policy of isolation America maintained

from world affairs since the late eighteenth century. The United States, thus, would no

longer remain idle towards regions threatened by communist influence. Second, NCS-68

identified a Soviet inclination for "proxy aggression"[51] rather than direct military

confrontation to destabilize the Western world. Truman's administration realized that the

United States needed conventional ground forces to defend international security.

The third major policy recommendation of NSC-68 focused on national defense.

America was technologically superior to the Soviet Union but inferior in military

personnel.[52] Therefore, Truman's administration sought increased defense spending to

increase America's conventional and nuclear military forces, and to help Western Europe

increase its defense capabilities.[53] Finally, NSC-68 recommended that the United States

eliminate previous security plans to defend select strongpoints, such as Japan in Asia, in

favor of defending across a wide perimeter. Therefore, differences between "peripheral

and vital interests"[54] no longer existed.

Truman's staff presented him with NSC-68 in April 1950. North Korea invaded

South Korea in June 1950. The Truman administration believed the invasion was Soviet

---

[50]Herring, *From Colony to Superpower: U.S. Foreign Relations since 1776*, 595.

[51]John Lewis Gaddis, *Strategies of Containment: A Critical Appraisal of Postwar American National Security Policy* (New York: Oxford University Press, 1982), 112.

[52]Ibid., 82.

[53]Herring, *From Colony to Superpower: U.S. Foreign Relations since 1776*, 638.

[54]Gaddis, *Strategies of Containment: A Critical Appraisal of Postwar American National Security Policy*, 92.

sponsored. Truman felt the DPRK was "obviously testing"[55] American resolve to contain communism by attacking South Korea. Thus, according to a majority of Truman's administration, North Korea's attack validated NSC-68's assumption regarding the United States' inability to rely solely on a nuclear deterrent against threats to global stability. Therefore, Truman's administration needed to increase considerably the size of America's conventional military forces to enforce the Truman Doctrine. However, Truman did not approve NSC-68's "basic approach" until September 30, 1950.[56] His delay was problematic. Specifically, his administration did not expect to create a credible offensive military capability through implementing NSC-68 until 1952.[57]

At the time of North Korea's invasion, the United States owned 50 percent of the world's wealth but six percent of its population.[58] The United States Army maintained only ten under strength divisions and eleven regimental combat teams on June 25, 1950.[59] Additionally, the Department of Defense positioned this small force in piecemeal form to meet security commitments in Western Europe and Japan. The United States,

[55]Truman, *Memoirs by Harry S. Truman, Volume II: Years of Trial and Hope*, 335.

[56]S. Nelson Drew, "Part I: Introduction. Paul Nitze and the Legacy of NSC-68," in *NSC-68: Forging the Strategy of Containment*, ed. S. Nelson Drew (Washington, DC: National Defense University Press, 1996), 2.

[57]U.S. National Security Council, A Report to the National Security Council by the Executive Secretary on United States Objectives and Programs for National Security, April 15, 1950, 32, Harry S. Truman Library, Independence, MO.

[58]U.S. Department of State, *Foreign Affairs of the United States 1948*, vol. 1, Part Two, 524.

[59]Russell F. Weigley, *The American Way of War: A History of United States Military Strategy and Policy* (Bloomington: Indiana University Press, 1973), 382.

thus, could supply immediately a substantial amount of military materiél to the conflict in Korea. However, its minimal supply of immediately available personnel limited the Truman administration's ability to send land forces to Korea.

The United States Air Force was America's only military arm immediately capable of responding to the invasion.[60] However, ground forces were required to repel decisively the communist attack in Korea. The United States, if one combines its reduced state of readiness and the dispersal of its land forces, clearly could not "go it alone"[61] in Korea in 1950, despite Truman's contrary claim after the war. Seeking to avoid identification as "the greatest appeasers of all time,"[62] Truman's administration resolved to make "democracy work against its enemies"[63] by requesting military support from members of the UN.

The ROK was "a ward of the United Nations . . . morally and legally"[64] after UN sponsored elections in 1948. Even if multinational contributions were "unimportant militarily,"[65] as Dean Acheson later claimed, they were "politically and

---

[60]Ibid.

[61]Merle Miller, *Plain Speaking: An Oral Biography of Harry S. Truman* (New York: G. P. Putnam's Sons, 1974), 276.

[62]Gaddis, *Strategies of Containment: A Critical Appraisal of Postwar American National Security Policy*, 112.

[63]National Archives and Records Service, *Public Papers of the Presidents of the United States: Harry S. Truman, 1950* (Washington, DC: Government Printing Office, 1965), 172.

[64]Richard P. Stebbins, *The United States in World Affairs, 1950* (New York: Harper & Brothers, 1951), 185.

[65]Acheson, *The Korean War*, 20.

psychologically"[66] significant to domestic American morale, and to a young UN organization still trying to establish its global credibility. Therefore, Truman's decision to turn South Korea's defense into a "decision for the United Nations itself"[67] through the contribution of combat forces from UN member nations was his best option.

It is at this point that the Truman administration's leadership during the Korean War becomes comparable to JP 3-16. The Truman administration developed an *ad hoc* organization for common action in Korea. Truman's leadership during the occupation of Japan provides an interesting precursor to its parallel in Korea. The occupation force in post-1945 Japan included American and Commonwealth forces.

The occupation force was an *ad hoc* organization. Truman used America's majority of troops in the occupation force to reserve for the United States the "controlling voice"[68] in Japan's administration. His position on this matter contrasts with JP 3-16's principles that advise coalition leaders to respect multinational contributions regardless of size and consider multinational perspectives when making decisions. Therefore, it is critical to analyze America's pre-1950 relationships with three key partners: Great Britain, Canada, and Australia.

Anglo-American relations during and after World War II are significant to the Korean War because Great Britain was America's most important partner during the

---

[66]Ibid.

[67]Miller, *Plain Speaking: An Oral Biography of Harry S. Truman*, 279.

[68]Harry S. Truman, *Memoirs by Harry S. Truman, Volume I: Year of Decisions* (Garden City, NY: Doubleday & Company, 1955), 455.

Second World War. The nations' "fraternal"[69] relationship leads one to believe that the equal partnership shared during World War II continued after 1945 and into the Korean War. However, the United States assumed undisputable leadership of the Western world, and for military operations in Korea, between 1945 and 1950. Thus, both nations managed their Korean War relationship from different positions of power than during World War II.

The United States entered World War II with fresh troops, new equipment, and a homeland undamaged by war. Germany and Japan threatened American interests in Europe and in the Pacific. Therefore, the United States viewed the Second World War as a global struggle. Conversely, Japan threatened British interests in the Pacific. However, Germany threatened directly Britain's "own life and survival"[70] before Adolf Hitler declared war on the United States.

Consequently, the British government prioritized operations against Germany over the "sideshow"[71] in the Pacific. Therefore, the United States and Great Britain did not always agree on war strategy. These facts are critical because British leaders knew they would have to "rely increasingly on American material aid"[72] to sustain their war effort. Although not publicly acknowledged by either nation, American entrance to the

---

[69]Fitzsimmons, *The Foreign Policy of the British Labour Government 1945-1951*, 121.

[70]Winston S. Churchill, *Victory. War Speeches by the Right Hon. Winston S. Churchill*, compiled by Charles Eade (Boston: Little, Brown and Company, 1946), 134.

[71]Dockrill, "The Foreign Office, Anglo-American Relations and the Korean War, June 1950-June 1951," 459.

[72]Anthony Eden, *The Reckoning* (Boston: Houghton Mifflin Company, 1965), 368.

war almost immediately set the stage for a transition of power and seniority within the Anglo-American partnership. This altered relationship continued after the war.

Franklin Roosevelt served as the United States President for the majority of America's participation in the Second World War. Winston Churchill served as Britain's Prime Minister until Germany surrendered. Dwight D. Eisenhower served as the Anglo-American's principle military commander. These three men brought the Anglo-American relationship as close as possible to "special" during World War II.

Churchill, for example, continually promoted Anglo-American unity as the only means to secure "the future of the whole world."[73] Neither Roosevelt nor Eisenhower outwardly utilized America's growing power to dominate their British partners. It is reasonable to conclude that Churchill enthusiastically supported this relationship because he understood his nation's growing dependence on the United States. Roosevelt appeared to understand the moral benefits of defeating Germany alongside Great Britain. Eisenhower also demonstrated an understanding of the positive effects inherent in an alliance.

However, Roosevelt died in 1945. Churchill, removed from office in 1945, was leader of the opposition in the House of Commons in 1950. He did not return to the Prime Minister's office until 1951. Eisenhower commanded the North Atlantic Treaty Organization (NATO) when North Korea invaded its southern neighbor. Therefore, a different set of personalities influenced Anglo-American relations from the end of World War II until June 1950. Similar and separate national interests influenced these personalities and shaped their relationship as the two nations transitioned into 1950.

---

[73]Churchill, *Blood, Sweat, and Tears*, 447.

However, the nature of the relations, with American in a dominant role, did not change significantly during this period.

Harry Truman and Clement Attlee occupied their nations' respective government leadership positions after World War II. Attlee was "anxious"[74] to continue the "special relationship" into the post-war period. Truman, on the other hand, "did not share this enthusiasm"[75] immediately after the war. Attlee found himself balancing efforts to gain Truman's favor and American assistance without creating the perception that he sought such assistance to sustain the British Empire. Global events changed Truman's opinions on Attlee, Great Britain, and America's role in the world. Instability in Greece and Turkey, the development of the Marshall Plan, British colonial goals, and control of atomic energy became critical components of their pre-Korean War relationship.

Britain's inability to reduce instability in Greece and Turkey forced Truman's administration to acknowledge the reliance of American security on British and Western European stability. Specifically, an economically unstable Great Britain, unable to project military force, increased the vulnerability of pre-1945 British regions of influence to Soviet aggression.[76] America would be required to fill all gaps left open by British limitations. However, Britain, along with post-war Western Europe, needed assistance to improve its ability to fulfill its role and obligations in defense of British and American security.

---

[74]Dockrill, *British Defence since 1945*, 23.

[75]Ibid.

[76]Robert H. Ferrell, ed., *Off the Record. The Private Papers of Harry S. Truman* (New York: Harper & Row, 1980), 104.

Truman reversed his previous position and identified Anglo-American unity as a "cornerstone"[77] of global stability. His administration secured approval of the Marshall Plan to provide economic assistance to, and to reduce instability, in Western Europe. The Marshall Plan was successful. However, it recreated an American pattern began during the Second World War. Specifically, United States officials recognized Britain's reliance on American support. Therefore, American representatives appeared to use this reality to secure British acceptance for American policies. Britain's political leaders understood their reliance on American support. However, British government officials sought to retain some sense of equality to their American counterparts while maintaining independence in thought and action. These interactions produced tension that most commonly arose from the Attlee government's efforts to retain a degree of Britain's pre-1945 influence in the world.

Truman's decision to insure the stability of the British Commonwealth did not imply an American blank check in support of all British actions. Indian independence, for example, created a problem for Anglo-American relations. Britain gained three specific benefits through its "enlightened"[78] colonization of India. First, Indian troops increased Britain's minimal supply of manpower times of war.[79] Second, military bases in India

---

[77]Truman, *Memoirs by Harry S. Truman, Volume II: Years of Trial and Hope*, 303.

[78]Sir Reader Bullard, *Britain and the Middle East: From Earliest Times to 1963* (London: Hutchinson University Library, 1964), 162.

[79]Dockrill, *British Defence since 1945*, 28.

allowed Britain to "shelter"[80] its interests in the "oil-bearing Middle East."[81] Third,

control of India provided an important market for British commerce.[82] India's

significance to Britain's stability after 1945 is obvious. Nevertheless, Attlee's

government understood that it could not retain India and granted independence in 1947.[83]

Truman did not present a united front with Attlee on India. Truman's position in

this example is confusing. He identified British stability as essential to American

security. Britain's control of India positively affected British stability. Truman's stance

on India reflected a growing assumption within his administration that American

assistance programs allowed his administration to remain support selectively British

interests. This knowledge continued to shape pre-1950 Anglo-American relations into the

Korean War, perhaps nowhere as significantly as in control of atomic energy.

Anglo-American cooperation for atomic energy nearly stopped after the American

Congress passed the 1946 McMahon Act. This Act illegalized the sharing of classified

atomic energy with foreign countries, including Great Britain.[84] Unfortunately, the Act

neglected several years of Anglo-American atomic development efforts and the combined

---

[80]Fitzsimmons, *The Foreign Policy of the British Labour Government 1945-1951*, 66.

[81]Thomas B. Millar, "Australia and the American Alliance," *Pacific Affairs* 37, no. 2 (Summer 1964): 149.

[82]John Kent, "Bevin's Imperialism and the Idea of Euro-Africa, 1945-49," in *British Foreign Policy, 1945-65*, ed. Michael Dockrill and John W. Young (New York: St. Martin's Press, 1989), 53.

[83]Dockrill, *British Defence since 1945*, 22.

[84]Margaret Gowing, "Britain, America, and the Bomb," in *British Foreign Policy, 1945-65*, ed. Michael Dockrill and John W. Young (New York: St. Martin's Press, 1989), 41.

Truman-Churchill decision to use atomic bombs against Japan.[85] Therefore, the McMahon Act removed Britain's co-equal status with the United States in an area of concern that was previously an equal Anglo-American effort. Furthermore, the McMahon Act inferred that Britain could not rely on America's atomic deterrent to defend purely British interests. These new conditions did not appear to concern Truman's administration until instability threatened Greece and Turkey.

Truman and his advisors nevertheless found it difficult to consider situations where "close contact with the British"[86] on atomic diplomacy did not exist. Regardless, Attlee's government, isolated from American atomic protection, decided to develop a British atomic bomb in 1946 to protect its nation's security.[87] This decision reflected the Attlee government's desire to maintain independence in thought and diplomacy wherever possible. Thus, national interests dominated the Anglo-American relationship from 1945-1950.

The British Commonwealth represented America's "most probable and most important allies"[88] in a war with the Soviet Union. Perceptions of Commonwealth reliability suggests that Truman's administration would seek Commonwealth support if major military operations occurred outside of Europe. North Korea's invasion of the

---

[85]Churchill, *Victory*, 293.

[86]U.S. Department of State, *Foreign Affairs of the United States 1948*, vol. 1, Part Two, 571.

[87]Dockrill, *British Defence since 1945*, 20-21.

[88]U.S. Department of State, *Foreign Relations of the United States, 1947, The British Commonwealth, Europe*, vol. 3 (Washington, DC: Government Printing Office, 1972), 593.

ROK presented a risk to American security interests in the Pacific. However, North Korea's invasion did not directly threaten British interests in the region. Specifically, North Korea's army could not immediately threaten British-controlled areas such as Hong Kong in June 1950.

Evidence suggests that Truman's administration did not reciprocate entirely the Attlee government's efforts to maintain the "special relationship" after 1945. Specifically, Anglo-American relations were not particularly "special" to Truman's administration until June 1950. Truman, therefore, could not rely on previous American assistance to gain British support for military operations in Korea. However, Truman needed partners willing and able to provide any available means to defeat North Korean aggression. His administration eventually secured British contributions. Canada was another nation from which Truman's administration pursued military contributions for Korea.

Three concerns highlighted the United States-Canadian relations after 1945. First, like Great Britain, security and economic development motivated Canada's diplomacy with the United States. Second, successive Canadian Prime Ministers sought to remove at least some British influence from their political decisions and orient closer to the United States. Third, Attlee's government attempted to maintain Britain's political hierarchy over Canada. Truman's administration appears to have pursued relations with Canada less from a position of superiority and more from a position of equality. This represents a difference to its relations with Great Britain. Economics and personalities appear to explain this difference.

William Lyon Mackenzie King, the Canadian Prime Minister during and after the Second World War, understood his nation could not remain dependent on Britain for military or economic support after 1945. Britain's finances were in shambles after the war. This status inhibited Britain's ability to trade or project military force in the world, and prompted Canada's government to seek closer economic ties to the United States. For example, Canadian exports to Great Britain shrank from 36 percent in 1939 to a mere 15 percent by 1946.[89] Conversely, Canadian exports to the United States rose from 40 percent to 69 percent during the same period. Economically, Canada became America's "best customer and foremost supplier."[90]

Significantly, Truman seemed friendlier with King than he did with Attlee. This appearance is possibly due to Truman's likely perception that King, unlike Attlee, was not seeking American financial assistance to revive a colonial empire. The Truman-King relationship thus presents itself as one built on mutual interests that equally supported the United States and Canada. Conversely, Attlee's government appeared to beg Truman's administration for assistance to support British interests. Several events and proposals between the King and Truman governments sought to enhance mutually their nations' post-war economic growth.

Truman and King continued the 1941 Hyde Park Agreement that combined American and Canadian economic resources in support of North America's continental

---

[89]John A. Stevenson, "Canada, Free and Dependent," *Foreign Affairs* 29, no. 3 (April 1951): 463.

[90]U.S. Department of State, *Foreign Relations of the United States, 1947,* vol. 3, 110.

defense.[91] Extending this pact shows that both leaders understood their mutual economic dependence because of their neighboring geographic locations. The extension also shows that both leaders, specifically Truman, were initially more concerned with homeland defense immediately after 1945 than with European security.

Militarily, American-Canadian relations after 1945 appeared to benefit both nations. For example, the North American neighbors began a personnel exchange program whereby each nation exchanged military officers to "increase the familiarity of each country's defense establishment with that of the other."[92] Additionally, the Canadian Parliament approved Recommendation 35 of the Permanent Joint Board of Defence, which "switched" Canada's weapons models from Britain to the United States.[93] This approval demonstrated the King government's realization of Canada's growing interdependence with the United States.

Canada was a nation with which the United States sustained a mutually supporting relationship after World War II. The two nations shared borders, were physically untouched by war, and maintained robust post-war economies. Interdependent economies, such as those shared between America and Canada, typically produce mutual security interests and, if required, military assistance. The proposals and events discussed reflect a united American-Canadian front for North American security. However, other

---

[91]Ibid.

[92]Ibid., 104.

[93]John C. Blaxland, "The Korean War: Reflections on Shared Australian and Canadian Military Experiences," *Canadian Military Journal* (Winter 2003-2004): 26.

conditions encouraged the Canadian governments to pursue greater ties to the United States.

Britain's ability to secure the British Commonwealth contributed significantly to its dominant role within that organization until 1945. However, it could not meet its pre-1945 commitments after 1945. Specifically, it could not guarantee Canada's security after World War II. Consequently, Britain lost its political dominance within the British Commonwealth after 1945. Conversely, the United States, as a "superpower," was capable of securing Canadian interests. Therefore, America's post-1945 status made it "almost inevitable that Washington should . . . replace London in the minds of the Canadian people and their government."[94] However, Canada continued to share interests with the British government.

Attlee's government created perhaps the greatest impediment to American-Canadian relations. It simultaneously sought to maintain its traditional authority within the Commonwealth and a high level of influence with Truman's administration "while denying the dominions any such advantage."[95] Thus, as Truman's administration moved to counter aggression throughout the world, the King and Louis St Laurent governments of Canada found themselves still heavily pulled towards Great Britain. Additionally, Truman's administration realized in 1947 that national defense "was best achieved as far

[94]Stevenson, "Canada, Free and Dependent," 460.

[95]Grey, *The Commonwealth Armies and the Korean War*, 2.

away"[96] from North America as possible. Its acknowledgement caused American-Canadian cooperation to suffer.

The purpose of discussing these events is to demonstrate America's unintended isolation after 1947. It was not isolated in the traditional sense whereby it avoided involvement in world affairs. Conversely, America's newfound ability and willingness to support democratic movements throughout the world, with or without capable international partners, explains its isolation in this example. Attlee's government frequently attempted to influence American diplomacy involving nations with historical links to Britain, such as Canada. Economic development, Attlee's priority after World War II, typically neglects military preparedness in favor of domestic stability. It appears that British decisions influenced Canadian thinking in this example. Thus, the Commonwealth's minimal military preparedness unintentionally isolated the United States.

Attlee's government clearly demonstrated that it considered itself the Truman administration's senior partner in global affairs. It found its Commonwealth hegemony challenged soon after the Second World War by an Australia whose war experiences changed Australia's perspective on Commonwealth membership.[97] Britain's military "weakness"[98] in the Pacific during World War II provoked Australia's government to

---

[96]Blaxland, "The Korean War: Reflections on Shared Australian and Canadian Military Experiences," 27.

[97]U.S. Department of State, *Foreign Relations of the United States, 1948: The Far East and Australia,* vol. 6 (Washington: Government Printing Office, 1974), 6.

[98]Fitzsimmons, *The Foreign Policy of the British Labour Government 1945-1951,* 19.

seek greater independence within the British Commonwealth and closer relations with the United States. Specifically, the international security environment changed, and Australian politicians knew that the United States could assure Australian security "far more efficiently" than British or Australian defense forces.[99] Thus, Australia's post-1945 relationships with Great Britain and the United States are worthy of review.

Australia's Prime Minister, Robert Menzies, did not want to remove Australia from the Commonwealth. However, he did want to prevent suggestions of Australian subordination to Great Britain.[100] Therefore, Menzies pursued a major post-war role in the Pacific theater to increase its independence within the Commonwealth.[101] He ensured that Australia represented the British Commonwealth on the Allied Council in Japan. Additionally, an Australian commanded the British Commonwealth Occupation Force area of responsibility in post-war Japan.[102] Furthermore, Menzies pursued a system in which, for example, Australia "would speak for the Commonwealth in Pacific affairs."[103] Finally, Menzies' government asserted itself as the "spokesman of the smaller and middle powers at the United Nations."[104]

---

[99]U.S. Department of State, *Foreign Relations of the United States, 1948*, vol. 6, 709.

[100]Ibid., 2.

[101]Grey, *The Commonwealth Armies and the Korean War*, 3.

[102]U.S. Department of State, *Foreign Relations of the United States, 1948*, vol. 6, 3.

[103]Ibid., 6.

[104]U.S. Department of State, *Foreign Relations of the United States, 1948*, vol. 6, 7.

Menzies employed Australia's tradition of designing its diplomatic and security policies "in relation to the great powers"[105] and chased a global leadership role for Australia independent of Attlee's government. His actions towards the Attlee government showed greater independence in action compared to his Canadian counterparts. He increased Australia's autonomy within the Commonwealth, raising his nation to a near-equal status regarding Great Britain, through its role in Japan. His acknowledgement of Britain's reduced capabilities spurred his pursuit of greater diplomatic and security relations with the Truman administration despite British efforts to remain America's dominant partner. King and St Laurent, on the other hand, appear content to uphold British positions on the international stage and assume that American protection was automatic, particularly after the creation of NATO.

Menzies displayed further independence in thought compared to King and St Laurent regarding Australian relations with the United States. His government, for example, pursued a security agreement with the United States equal to the North Atlantic Treaty agreement during 1945-1950. Truman, for his part, was willing to engage with any peoples "whose way of life and whose political ideology is similar to our own [*sic*]."[106] However, Menzies was not afraid to criticize American policies. His government feared a Japanese renewal of aggression in the Pacific.[107] Therefore, it was publicly critical of

---

[105]Harry G. Gelber, "Australia and the Great Powers," *Asian Survey* 15, no. 3 (March 1975): 191.

[106]U.S. Department of State, *Foreign Relations of the United States, 1948*, vol. 6, 1.

[107]Fitzsimmons, *The Foreign Policy of the British Labour Government 1945-1951*, 160.

American efforts to create a "U.S. bastion"[108] against the Soviet Union's eastern flank, and argued that Truman's administration should rebuild Japan's economy on Japanese merit and not for a purely political purpose.

Truman's administration found itself in an unenviable position. Many nations wanted closer economic, diplomatic, or security ties with the United States. However, nations seeking American support appeared unable or unwilling to provide something in return. Australia, for example, wanted a Pacific security pact. A Pacific security agreement without American participation, according to Australia's Minister for External affairs, was "unreal and meaningless."[109] Furthermore, Australia's pursuit of equal status with Great Britain within the Commonwealth likely increased the Attlee government's paternalism towards its "obstreperous children"[110] and its desire to maintain its status as the Truman administration's senior partner. Thus, Truman's administration received competing demands and requests without receiving much in return.

In comparison, Australian actions in pursuit of a Pacific security pact with America share similarities and differences with Canada's perception of its economic interdependence with the United States. In Canada, King and St Laurent understood that their national security was relatively safe given the American-Canadian border. If an attack occurred against American territory, for instance, the United States would likely

---

[108]U.S. Department of State, *Foreign Relations of the United States, 1948*, vol. 6, 4.

[109]Raymond Dennet and Robert K. Turner, ed., *Documents on American Foreign Relations, Vol. XII, January 1-December 31, 1950* (Princeton: Princeton University Press, 1951), 510.

[110]U.S. Department of State, *Foreign Relations of the United States, 1948*, vol. 6, 753.

assume a defensive posture that included Canadian borders. King and St Laurent, therefore, did not have anything to lose by not bowing to American diplomatic pressures.

Conversely, the United States did not base its Pacific security plan on Australian stability or security. Menzies' government, therefore, was in a position of having everything to gain by a security pact with the United States. However, it had much to lose if Truman's administration chose not to tie itself to Australian defense. These realities shaped events as Truman's administration developed a coalition for Korea. However, one example demonstrates mutual American-Commonwealth interests.

Truman's administration united with the Commonwealth governments to pursue collectively "an international control system"[111] for atomic energy. The Soviet Union put forth a proposal to the UN in 1948 that recommended international arms reductions. Additionally, the Soviets proposed that all nations reduce by one-third their military forces. Furthermore, they called for the prohibition of atomic weapons "as weapons intended for the aims of aggression and not for those of defense."[112] Soviet timing in this example is interesting because the United States remained the sole possessor of atomic weapons, and Soviet military forces surpassed in size the combined American, British, Canadian, and Australian forces.

The Western nations understood the hypocrisy of the Soviet's suggestion. However, they had to respond to the proposal lest the Soviets achieve a moral high

---

[111]U.S. Department of State, *Foreign Affairs of the United States 1948: General, The United Nations*, vol. 1, Part One (Washington: Government Printing Office, 1975), 417.

[112]Ibid., 431.

ground in Western public opinion.[113] Great Britain, Canada, and Australia specifically waited for a "strong, blunt"[114] speech from the United States before responding to the Soviet proposal. The Commonwealth's collective inclination to wait on an American response in times of uncertainty and political volatility after 1945, in addition to its economic and security concerns, demonstrated a disposition that waited for Truman's administration to take a lead position on important matters. The Commonwealth repeated this pattern of subordination to the United States after June 25, 1950.

Truman believed that the world was "closer to a permanent peace"[115] in June 1950 than at any time since 1945. North Korea's invasion of South Korea proved him incorrect. Truman and his advisors knew their military forces needed assistance to repel effectively North Korea's aggression. Unfortunately, they found in their allies political, economic, and military limitations. Additionally, Truman's administration perceived a strong Commonwealth willingness to let the United States assume "the lion's share"[116] of the burden. Therefore, Truman and Acheson required significant and insightful diplomatic measures to develop a coalition and meet the newest threat to world peace.

---

[113]Ibid., 456-457.

[114]Ibid., 457.

[115]National Archives and Records Service, *Public Papers of the Presidents of the United States: Harry S. Truman, 1950*, 450.

[116]Forrest C. Pogue, *George C. Marshall: Statesman, 1945-1959* (New York: Viking, 1987), 452.

CHAPTER 2

COALITION DEVELOPMENT

<u>Resolutions, Initial Actions, and Building a Coalition</u>

Dealing with an enemy is a simple and straightforward matter when contrasted
with securing close cooperation with an ally.
                    — Jeffrey Grey, The Commonwealth Armies and the Korean War

Examining three series of events explains the international environment following

the Democratic People's Republic of Korea's June 1950 invasion of the Republic of

Korea, and the appearance of British Commonwealth ground forces on the battlefield.

First, UN resolutions in response to the invasion demonstrated nearly unanimous

international support for South Korea's defense. Second, Harry Truman's efforts to

regulate initial American operations in Korea exhibited his administration's efforts to

procure multinational contributions to the war. Finally, Truman's administration

successfully developed a coalition to repel the communist invasion.

According to General Douglas MacArthur, the DPRK invasion was the first

communist "challenge to war against the free world."[117] MacArthur's comment ignored

activities, such as the Soviet Union's Berlin Blockade in 1948, in Europe. However,

North Korea's invasion resulted in the first UN operation in support of collective

security. The UN Security Council, absent the Soviet Union, unanimously passed an

American-sponsored cease-fire resolution a mere fifteen hours after identifying the

---

[117]Douglas MacArthur, *Reminiscences* (New York: Da Capo Press, 1964), 330.

invasion as more than a simple cross-border raid.[118] Two days later, the UN resolved to provide military assistance to the ROK. Only one member of the UN Security Council voted against this resolution. Six members of the UN General Assembly's 60 nations withheld support for the mandate that resolved to assist the ROK in an Assembly-wide vote.[119]

Supporters of the resolutions needed the Soviet Union to remain absent for the resolutions to receive approval. However, the near-unanimous approval of these resolutions demonstrated overwhelming UN-wide support for the ROK. It also showed that the majority of the world understood, as did the Truman administration, that North Korea's invasion was a "clear challenge"[120] to UN principles. The speed at which the UN approved these resolutions, and the overwhelming consent their approval received, suggested that UN members were willing and able to repel North Korea's invasion by providing immediate military assistance to South Korea. However, this was not true.

Members of the UN believed that the United States was the only nation capable of providing an immediate military response to defend the ROK. The British Commonwealth, for example, underwent a significant transformation between 1945 and 1950, whereby members such as Canada and Australia relied on American, rather than British, security assistance. Thus, the United States received informal responsibility to

---

[118]Building the Peace, Foreign Affairs Outlines no. 24, Autumn 1950, 1. Files of Charles Murphy, President's Secretary's Files, Papers of Harry S. Truman, Harry S. Truman Library, Independence, MO.

[119]Ibid., 2.

[120]U.S. Department of State, "The Conflict in Korea," *Far Eastern Series* 45, Pub. 4266 (Washington, DC: Government Printing Office, 1951), 12, Harry S. Truman Library, Independence, MO.

lead military operations in Korea. Additionally, non-communist nations assigned the United States "primary responsibility"[121] to execute the UN resolution. America's assignment provided Truman's administration with formal responsibility from a majority of the international community to lead military operations in Korea.

This assignment is justifiable with respect to one condition. The United States emerged from the Second World War as the West's superpower. Its military power, though reduced after World War II, still provided the West's most credible deterrent to communist aggression. These facts certainly justified the Truman administration's assignment to lead operations. However, the UN's apparent readiness to yield all responsibility for operations in Korea to the Truman administration revealed two critical considerations.

First, it presented a perception that UN members, having voted to support the ROK's defense, were unwilling to contribute their fair share of the forces necessary to accomplish the UN objective. It is reasonable to conclude that UN members preferred that the United States provide the majority of combat forces to Korea. One can also conclude that UN members hoped that the United States could accomplish quickly the mission in Korea before non-American troops, representing the UN, arrived. Second, it is logical to perceive that UN members were content to follow meekly the Truman administration's lead in Korea. Therefore, the Truman administration, receiving overwhelming support for its leadership, could conceivably conclude that UN members would follow willingly its leadership examples and decisions.

---

[121]U.S. Department of State, World Reaction to Korean Developments, Special Supplement, July 18, 1950, Harry S. Truman Library, Independence, MO.

The United States Congress authorized American combat troops for operations in Korea on June 30, 1950.[122] This approval occurred within 24 hours of the UN resolution in support of the ROK. Thomas E. Dewey, Truman's main opponent in the 1948 American presidential race, was among those who supported the Congress's authorization.[123] Dewey's nonpartisan support was representative of the substantial American domestic support for operations in Korea. Specifically, more than 80 percent of the United States supported operations in defense of South Korean sovereignty.[124]

The speed and nonpartisan nature with which the United States government responded to North Korea's invasion suggested that UN member nations merely had to follow the leader's example and provide military forces to operations in Korea. UN members overwhelmingly favored American leadership for military operations in Korea. The United States responded effectively to its UN-assigned responsibility. Additionally, non-communist members of the UN supported strongly the repelling of North Korean aggression. Therefore, it is reasonable to conclude that citizens of the British Commonwealth nations knew that the effort to save the ROK supported international, and not just American, interests. Thus, one can assume that these citizens, grateful for American military and economic assistance during and after World War II, would motivate their respective governments to return the favor.

---

[122]U.S. Department of State, Foreign Policy Studies Branch, Chronology of Principle Events Relating to the Korean Conflict, June-July 1950, 5, Harry S. Truman Library, Independence, MO.

[123]National Archives and Records Service, *Public Papers of the Presidents of the United States: Harry S. Truman, 1950*, 496.

[124]Gerald Astor, *Presidents at War: From Truman to Bush, the Gathering of Military Power to Our Commanders in Chief* (Hoboken, NJ: Wiley & Sons, 2006), 41.

The DPRK invasion presented a significant test to the Truman administration and the UN. Truman associated aggression in Korea with Greece's instability in 1947.[125] Specifically, Truman believed that a communist Korean peninsula threatened the security of American allies in the Pacific, such as Japan, and American credibility. Truman's decision to support Greece increased America's global commitments and, thus, its leadership and credibility in the non-communist world. Conversely, American inaction or incompetence in Korea, therefore, would reduce these distinctions.

American failures to respond effectively to the threat in Korea would also increase domestic criticism of the Truman administration's perceived weakness against communism. The United States Congress, for example, affixed substantial blame to Truman's administration for allowing communists to seize political power in China.[126] Efforts to respond to domestic criticism inspired the Truman administration's conduct as it developed a coalition for Korea. However, perhaps as important to Truman as American credibility, the UN needed military contributions from as many member nations as possible. Specifically, a successful military response would enhance the UN's credibility.

Truman correctly assessed the situation. The UN was a young organization in 1950. North Korea's invasion provided the UN with its first real opportunity to execute the role for which its founders intended. Therefore, immediate military support from member nations would enhance the organization's credibility and ensure its longevity. A

[125]President Truman's Conversation with George M. Elsey, June 26, 1950, Papers of George M. Elsey, Harry S. Truman Library, Independence, MO.

[126]Truman, *Memoirs by Harry S. Truman, Volume II: Years of Trial and Hope*, 430.

rapid military response that effectively repelled the DPRK invasion would only further enrich the UN's authority.

Conversely, minimal UN participation in Korea would present the organization as reliant on words rather than decisive action. Minimal UN participation in Korea would cause the organization's credibility to decline to the status its predecessor, the League of Nations, possessed during the 1930s.[127] Therefore, it is logical to assume that UN inaction in Korea would replicate the events that followed the League of Nations' failure to act after Germany began its conquest of Europe in 1939. The League's incompetence encouraged Adolf Hitler to act aggressively against his European neighbors and, therefore, created conditions that led to World War II.

Truman defined operations in Korea as a "police action."[128] Specifically, he defined the Korean War as something other than war. His explanation of operations in Korea was significant. A police action is comparable to limited war. In this form of warfare, political leaders establish objectives according to national interests, military capabilities, and a strong desire to avoid escalating the conflict.[129] Truman used the term "police action" to demonstrate his desire to the international community that he wanted to keep the war localized to Korea. Specifically, Truman defined operations in Korea as a police action to avoid escalating the war into a conflict with the Soviet Union or China.

---

[127]United Nations–Major Developments, April-June, July 5, 1950, 1. Papers of George M. Elsey, Harry S. Truman Library, Independence, MO.

[128]U.S. Department of State, White House Press and Radio News Conference, President Harry S. Truman, June 29, 1950, Harry S. Truman Library, Independence, MO.

[129]Ridgway, *The Korean War*, 245.

Truman's desire to avoid escalation in Korea was evident. For example, he denied requests from his military leaders to conduct aerial reconnaissance over the DPRK if those missions risked flying over Soviet or Chinese territory.[130] Reconnaissance flights over the Soviet Union or China were provocative in nature. Therefore, conducting aerial flights over either nation would prompt Soviet or Chinese military involvement in Korea. Additionally, Truman wanted the DPRK Army destroyed "to the maximum extent possible"[131] before UN forces reached the 38th Parallel. Achieving this goal would keep the war localized to Korea and reduce the potential for Soviet or Chinese intervention.

Truman's guidance is justified for two reasons. First, the limitations he imposed acknowledged UN fears of operations in Korea escalating into a general war with the Soviet Union or China.[132] Soviet military participation in Korea, for example, could prompt Soviet leaders to make war in Europe. Additionally, initial American forces sent to Korea were incapable of defeating either nation in Korea. Furthermore, Truman could not depend on his European allies to make war simultaneously in Korea and in Europe. Second, Truman's guidance sufficiently reassured American allies that war in Korea would not distract America's focus and military forces from Europe.[133] Truman's

---

[130]U.S. Department of State, Memorandum of Conversation, Dean Rusk (Assistant Secretary of State) and Brigadier General P. Hamilton, U.S. Air Force, July 6, 1950, Harry S. Truman Library, Independence, MO.

[131]Memorandum of Conversation, U.S./U.K. Discussions on Present World Situation, 20-24 July 1950, General Omar Bradley, Ambassador Phillip C. Jessup and Sir Oliver Franks, Lord Tedder, Harry S. Truman Library, Independence, MO.

[132]James with Wells, *Refighting the Last War: Command and Crisis in Korea, 1950-1953*, 1.

[133]Dockrill, *British Defence since 1945*, 42.

regulations enhanced the credibility of his stated goal to defend the UN charter and adhere to American security commitments.

Unfortunately, however, Truman's guidance unintentionally inferred that he did not want to place sufficient priority on operations in Korea in June 1950. His initial response to the DPRK invasion was strong. Nevertheless, Truman's guidance demonstrated the potential for his Europe-first security strategy to reduce American contributions to Korea. One can logically conclude that the Commonwealth would willingly follow the American example in this instance. Specifically, it is reasonable to believe that Commonwealth governments would resist American or UN pressures to provide substantial forces for Korea when the United States provided a small force. Sadly, the initial performance of the Eighth United States Army (EUSA) failed to encourage UN military contributions.

Truman's administration rushed EUSA units from Japan to repel North Korea's invasion. EUSA faced conditions in Korea that resembled general war instead of a "police action." Additionally, its leaders did not expect to complete an organizational combat readiness certification program until the end of July 1950.[134] Therefore America's initial forces in Korea were substantially unprepared for combat in June 1950, and found themselves almost immediately at severe risk for expulsion from the peninsula. Thus, the Truman administration's best methods to accomplish the UN mandate included limiting the scope in Korea and increasing the size of the UN Command through multinational contributions.

---

[134]Hanson, *Combat Ready? The Eighth U.S. Army on the Eve of the Korean War*, 18.

The Truman administration's prompt response in Korea demonstrated to its allies its intention to contain communism.[135] However, EUSA's poor performance increased the allies' doubts about America's ability to defend them.[136] Specifically, America's European allies questioned how the United States could effectively deter or defeat Soviet aggression in Europe if American forces could not defeat a smaller and less-capable army in Korea. Therefore, it is conceivable to conclude that EUSA's initial incompetence forced Commonwealth governments to reconsider any thoughts of sending their own military forces to Korea.

Evidence supports this conclusion. The Commonwealth governments continuously received "grim news"[137] of the UN Command's predicament in July 1950. British, Canadian, and Australian governments wanted "some idea of the American plan"[138] to change the circumstances in Korea. However, Commonwealth nations had their own combat limitations at this time.

The Commonwealth nations' lack of preparation for combat paralleled the United States Army's level of military unpreparedness. Nevertheless, domestic and international considerations motivated the Truman administration's conduct after it decided to send military forces to Korea. Therefore, it wanted its UN partners to contribute land forces to

---

[135]Memorandum of Conversation, Cabinet Meeting, July 14, 1950, Papers of Dean Acheson, Harry S. Truman Library, Independence, MO.

[136]U.S. Department of State, World Reaction to Korean Developments, Special Supplement, July 18, 1950, Harry S. Truman Library, Independence, MO.

[137]William Johnston, *A War of Patrols: Canadian Army Operations in Korea* (Vancouver: UBC Press, 2003), 23.

[138]Anthony Farrar-Hockley, *The British Part in the Korean War, Volume I: A Distant Obligation* (London: Her Majesty's Stationary Office, 1990), 53.

Korea. UN contributions of ground forces, even if "just a company or two,"[139] could accomplish two American goals.

First, UN contributions of land forces to Korea would sustain American domestic support for the war by showing the American public that theirs was not the only nation supporting Korea. Additionally, UN contributions would demonstrate the Truman administration's effective leadership to its domestic audience. Second, UN military contributions could enhance the UN Command's ability to achieve the goals of the UN mandates. Forces from as many nations as possible created conditions for more aggressive military operations. Thus, the Truman administration pursued military contributions from the UN. Specifically, it sought contributions from Great Britain, Canada, and Australia.

The Truman administration identified Great Britain in 1950 as its "only really dependable ally."[140] The Anglo-American partnership during the Second War likely created this perception. Yet, Britain's government, led by Clement Attlee, decided to support its ally with the ground forces it desperately needed one full month after the DPRK invasion. However, one should not assume that Attlee's government was merely content to let the United States shoulder the combat burden in Korea or lacked the political will to uphold UN mandates. Attlee's government had valid reasons for delaying its decision to send forces to Korea.

---

[139]President's Meeting with Congressional Leaders, July 30, 1950, 9. Papers of George M. Elsey, Harry S. Truman Library, Independence, MO.

[140]Robert O'Neill, *Australia in the Korean War 1950-53. Volume I: Strategy and Diplomacy* (Canberra: Australian Government Publishing Service, 1981), 69.

Attlee's government faced national security concerns other than upholding UN credibility in Korea in 1950. Chiefly, it was concerned about Western Europe's security. Additionally, the vulnerability of British areas of responsibility such as Greece and Malaya to Soviet influence concerned Attlee's government.[141] Attlee's government stationed a substantial number of soldiers in those areas to defeat communist threats to their stability. Additionally, it maintained a significant contingent of British infantry in Hong Kong to defend that possession.[142]

The ability of Attlee's government to provide land forces to Korea was clearly limited. Additionally, Attlee's government needed Britain's military power to respond to direct threats to British interests. The Malayan Communist Party, for example, "sought to overthrow the British colonial administration"[143] in Malaya. This outcome was unacceptable for any British government and, therefore, required military forces to negate the communist threat.

Furthermore, Attlee's government still required significant economic assistance from external sources to recover from the Second World War. Attlee's government, therefore, viewed Hong Kong as an asset to stimulate Britain's economic recovery. Thus, the Attlee government needed to dedicate sufficient forces to secure that possession. British commitments, therefore, reflected a nation with minimal capability to send forces

---

[141]Message from Mr. Attlee to the President, July 6, 1950, Harry S. Truman Library, Independence, MO.

[142]Fitzsimmons, *The Foreign Policy of the British Labour Government 1945-1951*, 136.

[143]Richard Stubbs, "From Search and Destroy to Hearts and Minds: The Evolution of British Strategy in Malaya 1948-60," in *Counterinsurgency in Modern Warfare*, ed. Daniel Marston and Carter Malkasian (Oxford: Osprey Publishing, 2010), 101.

elsewhere. A large British commitment to Korea would further strain Britain's poor economic situation. According to Attlee's government, Britain could only make a small contribution to the UN command in 1950.

However, Dean Acheson wanted the British to "set a good pattern"[144] for other nations by contributing ground forces. He strongly urged Sir Oliver Franks, Britain's ambassador to the United States, to encourage his government to provide troops earlier than the two months Attlee's government considered possible.[145] Acheson did not understand or completely disregarded Britain's limitations.

Acheson's demands on Britain exhibited three considerations. First, they demonstrated his expectations for an automatic contribution of British ground forces to Korea. Second, Acheson's demands suggested that he expected the British to contribute forces to Korea simply because they were an American ally in Europe. Third, Acheson's demands reflected a belief that American economic and military assistance for Britain after 1945 obligated Attlee's government to contribute combat forces to Korea.

Acheson's behavior towards Franks did not reflect knowledge or understanding of a potential coalition partner's capabilities and limitations. Additionally, Acheson ignored the national economic effects on an ally's contributions to the cause for which that alliance was established. Specifically, Acheson ignored Britain's significant economic

---

[144]Memorandum of Conversation: Proposed UK Note Relating to Increased Military Effort; China, Dean Acheson and Sir Oliver Franks, August 3, 1950, 2. Papers of Dean Acheson, Harry S. Truman Library, Independence, MO.

[145]U.S. Department of State, World Reaction to Korean Developments, No. 30, July 27, 1950, Harry S. Truman Library, Independence, MO.

and military investments in the NATO. Finally, his demands made previous American assistance to its allies appear conditional to future American demands.

Acheson's diplomacy, however one-sided, stimulated the British government to contribute military forces to Korea. Attlee knew that his nation depended on American security in Europe. Two British battalions arrived to Korea on August 29, 1950.[146] These forces arrived within a month of Britain's approval to send ground forces. Thus, they arrived ahead of the two-month timeline projected by Franks. Furthermore, Britain provided nine operational naval vessels and promised a Marine Commando unit for Korea by September 1, 1950. By October 6, 1950, 19 British naval ships supported operations in Korea. Additionally, Attlee's government promised to place a brigade of 7700 troops, including the two battalions already in Korea, on the peninsula by the middle of November.[147] The British 29th Infantry Brigade arrived to Korea on November 3, 1950 to complete Britain's initial force contributions.[148]

Attlee anxiously sought to prove his nation's "credentials as a close ally of the United States."[149] He supported this objective by making Britain the first UN member nation after the United States to place ground troops in Korea. Furthermore, Attlee's commitment of naval support removed some responsibility from the Truman

---

[146]Status of United Nations Military Assistance Offers, September 1, 1950, 1. President's Secretary's Files, Harry S. Truman Library, Independence, MO.

[147]Status of United Nations Military Assistance Offers, October 6, 1950, 1. President's Secretary's Files, Harry S. Truman Library, Independence, MO.

[148]U.S. Department of State, Foreign Policy Studies Branch, Chronology of Principle Events Relating to the Korean Conflict, November 1950, iv. Harry S. Truman Library, Independence, MO.

[149]Dockrill, *British Defence since 1945*, 43.

administration to allocate forces to naval operations. However, diverging interests between the two allies arose soon after Britain's forces arrived in Korea.

Attlee understood that his nation's responsibilities to Greece, Malaya, and Hong Kong limited its capabilities for Korea. Nevertheless, he told his nation to "gird itself for the necessary economic sacrifices"[150] in response to Britain's contributions to Korea. Attlee's comment in the face of Britain's substantial commitments demonstrated his solidarity with the Truman administration. However, Attlee's government continuously warned the Truman administration about becoming too involved in Korea at the expense of its credible deterrent to Soviet aggression in Europe or the Middle East.[151] Truman's continuous emphasis on his goal to limit the war to Korea appears to have remained unnoticed. Additionally, Attlee's efforts to use his self-perceived influence with Truman, in conjunction with Dean Acheson's methods of diplomacy, created three problems in Anglo-American diplomacy.

United Nations' objectives in Korea constituted the first difficulty. Attlee's government frequently expressed its desire for the war to remain localized to Korea.[152] "Localized" meant that UN forces fought only DPRK forces in Korea. Attlee's government appeared to reverse this position by proposing a UN resolution, approved on

---

[150]U.S. Department of State, *Foreign Relations of the United States 1950,* vol. 3, 1386.

[151]U.S. Department of State, World Reaction to Korean Developments, No. 28, July 25, 1950, Harry S. Truman Library, Independence, MO.

[152]U.S. Department of State, Memorandum of Conversation, U.S.-U.K. Discussions on Present World Situation, 20-24 July 1950, General Omar Bradley, Ambassador Phillip C. Jessup and Sir Oliver Franks, Lord Tedder, Harry S. Truman Library, Independence, MO.

October 7, 1950, that sought a "unified, independent and democratic Government in the Sovereign State of Korea."[153]

The UN's objective on June 25, 1950 was to restore the ROK government. Attempting to unify all of Korea changed this objective. China's Premier, Zhou Enlai, was already warning by October 1 that China "would not stand aside"[154] if UN forces advanced into North Korea. Attlee's proposed resolution, thus, made war with China expected rather than possible.

Attlee's proposal to unify Korea deviated from Truman's goal to keep the war localized and avoid a larger war in Korea with either the Soviet Union or China. Attlee's suggestion was particularly unsound if one considers that Acheson's belief that the size of a coalition partner's contribution regulated its ability to recommend policy changes. Attlee's government, in Acheson's perspective, did not contribute sufficient forces to Korea to warrant a significant voice in determining policy. Acheson's perspective, thus, contributed to the second difficulty between the allies and coalition partners.

Acheson constantly referred to American majorities in personnel and materiél to justify his nation's retention of decision-making responsibility. American dominance in these areas led officials like Acheson to consider compromise as unnecessary to coalition development or sustainment. For example, UN forces clearly needed multinational troops to enhance the organization's credibility and sustain domestic American support for the

---

[153]Fitzsimmons, *The Foreign Policy of the British Labour Government 1945-1951*, 136.

[154]U.S. Department of State, Foreign Policy Studies Branch, Chronology of Principle Events Relating to the Korean Conflict, September 1950, ii.

war. However, Acheson used American preponderance to demand more ground forces from coalition partners without considering those partners' limitations.

Acheson's demands were especially frequent in the war's early months. Sir Oliver Franks particularly disliked Acheson's use of a percentage-based system to define the size and significance of a nation's contribution levels. Specifically, Franks believed this method "did not do justice" to Britain's contributions.[155] Therefore, Franks' argument suggests Acheson's lack of understanding of, and patience for, partner limitations.

The United States provided 95 percent of the UN's military and financial burdens in Korea.[156] Therefore, Acheson's viewpoint is understandable from an American perspective. However, coalitions do not revolve around the wishes of one nation. Political leaders develop coalitions for specific reasons. Such reasons include, but are not limited to, desires for an operation to gain legitimacy from the international community.

International legitimacy encourages conditions for a politician's electorate to support the operation. George H.W. Bush's administration, for example, developed a coalition to conduct Operation Desert Shield/Desert Storm to legitimize operations in Iraq to the American public and the international community. However, Bush's administration did not use American military dominance to demand its coalition partners' blind adherence to American desires. Acheson acted in the opposite manner. His

---

[155]U.S. Department of State, Memorandum of Conversation: Proposed UK Note Relating to Increased Military Effort; China, Dean Acheson and Sir Oliver Franks, August 3, 1950, 1. Papers of Dean Acheson, Harry S. Truman Library, Independence, MO.

[156]O'Neill, *Australia in the Korean War 1950-53. Volume I: Strategy and Diplomacy*, 343.

percentage-based method of determining contribution significance and unremitting insistence for additional ground forces created the coalition partners' third difficulty.

In 1950, Attlee wanted to reestablish the level of influence his nation held with the United States during the Second World War.[157] He sought to establish an Anglo-American military committee to determine operations for Korea as a means to accomplish this goal. United States leaders such as General Omar Bradley rejected Attlee's proposal.[158] Bradley, for example, argued that committees could not run wars.[159] Interestingly, Bradley and his counterparts ignored the American experience in Europe during World War II. Specifically, General Dwight D. Eisenhower received orders for the European theater from the Anglo-American Combined Chiefs of Staff throughout the Second World War. Therefore, the United States and Great Britain utilized a committee approach to make war in Europe.

Truman's administration clearly felt that its men and materiél dominance justified their retaining undisputed leadership in Korea. However, the UN sanctioned the United States' lead in Korean operations. The coalition in Korea, therefore, operated within a "lead nation" command structure. Under this structure, one nation retains command and control over all coalition forces.[160] Lead nation command structures are unfeasible if two

---

[157]Jeffrey Grey, *The Commonwealth Armies and the Korean War* (Manchester, UK: Manchester University Press, 1988), 2.

[158]U.S. Department of State, Memorandum of Conversation, General Omar Bradley, Ambassador Phillip C. Jessup, July 12, 1950.

[159]U.S. Department of State, *Foreign Relations of the United States 1950,* vol. 3, 1760.

[160]Chairman, Joint Chiefs of Staff, Joint Publication 3-16 (2007), xii.

or more nations share command and control responsibilities. Therefore, it is reasonable to forgive Truman's administration for refusing Attlee's committee-based approach because the UN assigned to the United States, and no other nation, primary responsibility for the Korean War.

Command structures in Attlee's desired form are either integrated structures, as seen in the Second World War, or a parallel structure. A parallel command structure operates without a designated force commander.[161] Constitutionally, the Truman administration could not allow American forces to operate without a designated commander. However, United States dominance in men and materiél, which created part of its disinterest in an integrated structure, could have encouraged Attlee and other allies to increase British contributions to operations in Korea.

It appears that Truman's administration did not consider the possible effects of its effort to retain its lead-nation status in Korea on Anglo-American relations during or after the Korean War. This inconsideration is problematic because it created tension between Truman's administration and the Commonwealth governments that affected post-war diplomacy. Furthermore, Attlee increased this tension by seeking a high level of influence with the Truman administration while denying "any such advantage"[162] to British Commonwealth nations such as Canada and Australia.

Attlee's efforts to restrict Commonwealth influence with the Truman administration appear not to have affected initially Canada's Louis St Laurent government. St Laurent wanted any Canadian force sent to Korea to fight as part of a

---

[161]Ibid., xii.

[162]Grey, *The Commonwealth Armies and the Korean War*, 2.

Commonwealth organization. St Laurent desired this status so that Canada could use British supply lines and reduce its war-related expenses.[163] Furthermore, he wanted the UN's "formal involvement"[164] for all combat-related decisions.

St Laurent's general aims aligned with specific American and British objectives for Korea. He understood that multinational participation enhanced the UN's credibility. Furthermore, St Laurent supported Truman's goal to limit the war to Korea. He believed that a limited war in Korea would "pay an insurance premium that will be far less costly than the losses we would face if a new conflagration devastated the world."[165]

St Laurent, like Truman and Attlee, correctly understood that a war to contain communism in Korea would likely be less costly in terms of casualties and finances than a general war with the Soviet Union in Europe. St Laurent's nation shared an interdependent economy with the United States. Additionally, Canada's homeland security relied heavily on American assistance. Given the commonalities in war and peace, and a direct reliance on American support, it is reasonable to expect that St Laurent's government immediately offered to contribute available military forces to the American-led coalition in Korea. However, this did not happen.

---

[163]Brent Byron Watson, *Far Eastern Tour: The Canadian Infantry in Korea, 1950-1953* (Montreal: McGill-Queen's University Press, 2002), 33.

[164]Blaxland, "The Korean War: Reflections on Shared Australian and Canadian Military Experiences," 27.

[165]James Eayrs, *In Defence of Canada: Growing Up Allied* (Toronto: University of Toronto Press, 1980), 62.

Interestingly, St Laurent's government wanted requests for Canadian ground forces to come from the UN rather than the United States.[166] Three possible reasons explain this wish. First, St Laurent genuinely wanted the UN organization to succeed. This reason sensibly explains his wish. The UN could succeed by demonstrating leadership in Korea. UN requests for combat troops would portray an organization that accepted its responsibilities and exhibited leadership. Furthermore, greater UN ownership of the coalition, demonstrated through UN-based requests for combat forces, would enhance the organization's overall credibility. However, St Laurent's second possible reason for wanting contribution requests to come from the UN is perhaps more practical.

Canada had "no troops available"[167] for Korea in June or July of 1950. Additionally, St Laurent's government had yet to station Canada's "obligatory Brigade" in Europe as part of NATO by June 1950.[168] St Laurent likely knew of Acheson's treatment of Franks. Therefore, it is conceivable that he did not want his diplomats to receive similar treatment. It is reasonable to conclude that St Laurent believed that American requests were likely to be more confrontational and less understanding of Canadian limitations than UN requests. Furthermore, given to Canada's inability to meet its NATO obligations and its reliance on American security assistance, American-based requests for would likely be less easy for St Laurent to refuse.

---

[166]U.S. Department of State, World Reaction to President's Statement, No. 2, June 29, 1950, Harry S. Truman Library, Independence, MO.

[167]Memorandum of Conversation: Formosa; Contribution of Troops by Canada, Dean Acheson and Lester B. Pearson, July 29, 1950, Papers of Dean Acheson, Harry S. Truman Library, Independence, MO.

[168]Grey, *The Commonwealth Armies and the Korean War*, 31.

Canada's contributions to the world at large paled in comparison to Great Britain's efforts. Therefore, Acheson's treatment of Franks makes it feasible to believe that Acheson would use Canada's non-adherence to its NATO obligations to demand Canadian ground forces for Korea. One can easily see Acheson demand that Canada fulfill its obligations somewhere regardless of location. The initial priority that Truman's administration placed on Korea over other commitments, such as NATO, indicated that Acheson preferred that Canadian forces join the UN coalition in Korea. Therefore, it is reasonable to conclude that Canada's lack of available troops was St Laurent's primary reason for wanting troop requests to come from the UN.

Widespread popular Canadian support for the UN' Korean resolutions also likely affected the Truman administration's diplomacy with St Laurent's government. Canada's *Globe and Mail* newspaper, for example, recommended an immediate contribution of Canadian troops to demonstrate that St Laurent's government "at last acknowledges this country's duty"[169] to the international community beyond NATO and peacekeeping operations.[170] Furthermore, public opinion polls showed that Canadians strongly supported the Truman administration's quick and decisive response to the DPRK invasion.[171]

Strong Canadian support for operations in Korea, thus, likely prompted Dean Acheson to treat claims by St Laurent's government that it could not provide immediate

---

[169]Watson, *Far Eastern Tour: The Canadian Infantry in Korea, 1950-1953*, 6.

[170]Blaxland, "The Korean War: Reflections on Shared Australian and Canadian Military Experiences," 25.

[171]John Melady, *Korea: Canada's Forgotten War* (Toronto: MacMillan of Canada, 1983), 29.

ground forces to Korea with perhaps more contempt than that with which he treated similar claims from Great Britain. For example, Acheson told Lester Pearson, Canada's Minister for External Affairs, "quite forcibly" that the UN mission in Korea was of such importance that it required all nations "contribute as much as they could to the United Nations effort."[172] Regardless of domestic support, this manner of diplomacy is unlikely to gain a potential partner's commitment of forces.

Acheson's desire for multiple UN member nations to contribute ground forces is understandable. Contributions from a significant number of member nations would validate the UN's resolutions for Korea and increase its credibility. A coalition comprised of American and ROK soldiers, on the other hand, would not enhance UN credibility. Operations in this circumstance would support communist claims of the United States' responsibility for the aggression in Korea.

Acheson's expectations for Canadian contributions to Korea is understandable given Canada's, compared to America's or Great Britain's, limited worldwide commitments. The United States and Great Britain supplied troops to NATO and met numerous security commitments throughout the world. Canada did not perform either of these tasks. Acheson's condescending tone, however, leads one to question why other nations would willingly submit their forces to American leadership in Korea if their diplomats, and possibly their soldiers, were to receive Acheson's harsh approach to diplomacy. Furthermore, Acheson's diplomatic methods lead one to question his mental state.

---

[172]Memorandum of Conversation: Formosa; Contribution of Troops by Canada, Dean Acheson and Lester B. Pearson, July 29, 1950, Papers of Dean Acheson, Harry S. Truman Library, Independence, MO.

Dean Acheson's actions presented three considerations. First, it is possible that Acheson lacked an accurate understanding of Canada's limitations. Second, Acheson appeared to exhibit a belief that Truman's administration could dictate terms and policies to its potential coalition partners and its allies. Third, it is likely that Acheson's tactics created a Commonwealth perception that believed the Truman administration would continue its harsh diplomacy after the Korean War. These possibilities were critical. Specifically, they threatened American diplomacy with its allies and coalition partners after the Korean War. Furthermore, they may possibly have reduced America's position of moral leadership in the non-communist world.

Speaking "forcibly" is not a manner to engender contributions from a potential coalition partner. Furthermore, it is a poor manner with which to engage allies. St Laurent's government was primarily responsible for ensuring the safety and welfare of all Canadians. It never signed an agreement to provide military forces to participate in UN military operations. Canada's limitations, whether or not Acheson perceived them as real, were valid to St Laurent's government. Therefore, Acheson's tactics stimulated resentment from the St Laurent government for Truman's administration.

St Laurent announced on July 19, 1950 that the "dispatch of Canadian Army units to the Far East was not warranted."[173] William Lyon Mackenzie King, St Laurent's predecessor, died soon after this announcement, and St Laurent's entire cabinet attended King's funeral. While returning to Ottawa from the funeral, St Laurent and his cabinet decided to send military forces to Korea.[174] St Laurent announced that Canadian military

---

[173]Watson, *Far Eastern Tour: The Canadian Infantry in Korea, 1950-1953*, 6.

[174]Melady, *Korea: Canada's Forgotten War*, 37.

forces would participate in Korea on August 7, 1950.[175] St Laurent overturned his initial

inclination less than three weeks after his first announcement. Four possible reasons exist

to explain why St Laurent's government reversed its original position.

First, King's close relationship with Truman likely assisted the cabinet's decision

to provide forces to Korea. King and Truman pursued several avenues of mutual interest

after World War II until St Laurent became Canada's Prime Minister. For example,

Truman and King extended the 1941 Hyde Park Agreement to combine their nations'

resources in support of North America's continental defense.[176] They also implemented

methods to improve their respective military's familiarity with each other.[177] Sources on

deliberations within St Laurent's government do not identify King's close relationship

with Truman as a primary source of its turnaround. However, the cabinet decided to send

forces after attending King's funeral. Therefore, it is feasible to conclude that St

Laurent's government wanted to avoid damaging its relationship with the United States

by an inability or unwillingness to send forces to Korea.

Clement Attlee's announcement of British force contributions occurred before St

Laurent announced that Canadian forces would participate in Korea.[178] Therefore,

Attlee's timing provides a second possible cause behind the Canadian government's

reversal. Britain's limited ability to support operations in Korea did not stop Attlee's

---

[175]Watson, *Far Eastern Tour: The Canadian Infantry in Korea, 1950-1953*, 6.

[176]U.S. Department of State, *Foreign Relations of the United States, 1947,* vol. 3, 110.

[177]Ibid., 104.

[178]O'Neill, *Australia in the Korean War 1950-53, Volume I: Strategy and Diplomacy*, 93.

government from supporting its American ally. St Laurent could not hope to maintain favor with the American or British governments by failing to contribute Canadian forces.

Acheson's harsh diplomacy likely helped remind St Laurent's government of this consideration. Tactics from the American Secretary of State, thus, constitute the third possible reason behind St Laurent's decision to provide Canadian forces to the UN Command. Finally, domestic Canadian support for the ROK's defense provides the fourth possible reason for St Laurent's shift. Canadian newspapers and opinion polls showed support for the Truman administration and the UN mandate. Therefore, St Laurent, who likely wanted to continue serving as Canada's Prime Minister, had to consider his constituents' opinions.

Naval forces and an air capability, however, remained the only contributions Canada could immediately provide to a UN coalition that still "urgently needed"[179] land forces during August and September 1950. By September 1, 1950, Canada placed three naval destroyers under the UN command. Additionally, it provided a squadron of the Royal Canadian Air Force to transport American soldiers from North America to Korea.[180] St Laurent's government formally offered an infantry brigade of 6500 soldiers on August 14.

St Laurent formally offered land forces one week after his announcement that Canada would support Korean operations. Pressure from people like Acheson continued

---

[179]U.S. Department of State, Report of the United Nations Command Operations in Korea for the period 16-31 August 1950, transmitted by Ambassador Warren R. Austin, U.S. Representative to the United Nations, to the President of the Security Council, September 18, 1950, 8. Harry S. Truman Library, Independence, MO.

[180]Status of United Nations Military Assistance Offers, September 1, 1950, 1.

to remind St Laurent's government that its contributions were insufficient. Therefore, St Laurent's government hastened the deployment timeline of the 2nd Battalion, Princess Patricia's Canadian Light Infantry (2 PPCLI) to Korea to answer its critics. However, factors other than international criticism also appear to have motivated St Laurent's decision to rush this deployment.

Canadian ground forces had yet to reach Korea when the Inchon landings occurred. The post-Inchon offensive was successful enough to suggest that the war could soon be over.[181] Canada could not claim any of the credit for victory if this occurred. As a result, the Canadian government would not have a voice in a post-war occupation administration, and Canada would likely lose credibility and respect as a NATO ally. Moreover, St Laurent would find his government's influence within the British Commonwealth diminished. Furthermore, failure to contribute ground troops would likely harm Canada's security reliance on the United States. Therefore, one can reasonably conclude that political reasons motivated the accelerated deployment of Canadian land forces to Korea

Canada's air squadron did not meet Truman or Acheson's demands for ground forces, but they were ignoring the critical fact that the Canadians were transporting American soldiers to Korea. Air transportation is a seemingly insignificant and easy task; however, its importance to combat operations is significant because it gets soldiers to the battlefield. Therefore, air transportation became a mission that did not require American personnel or equipment. Thus, Canada's air contribution enabled the Truman administration to concentrate American air power on combat operations rather than

---

[181]Melady, *Korea: Canada's Forgotten War*, 47.

ancillary tasks. Nevertheless, Acheson continued his effort to force on St Laurent's

government a realization that it "ought to do what Australia . . . had done."[182]

Australia was perhaps even more limited from a manpower perspective in 1950

than Canada. Its army, for example, maintained a mere 14,651 troops on active duty in

June 1950.[183] Furthermore, the Australian Army was the "main Commonwealth prop"[184]

in the Middle East and still had occupation forces in Japan.[185] Therefore, it was more

occupied than the Canadian Army with international commitments. However, Australia

contributed forces to Korea almost immediately. Consequently, Australian contributions

were more "well-publicized" in the United States than Canadian contributions.[186]

Australia's assistance took time to materialize but had "a positive diplomatic effect"[187] on

its relations with the United States.

Truman's administration did not treat Menzies' government with the harsh

diplomacy it employed against the Attlee and St Laurent governments. Two possible

---

[182]Memorandum of Conversation: Formosa; Contribution of Troops by Canada, Dean Acheson and Lester B. Pearson, July 29, 1950, Papers of Dean Acheson, Harry S. Truman Library, Independence, MO.

[183]Blaxland, "The Korean War: Reflections on Shared Australian and Canadian Military Experiences," 27.

[184]Geoffrey Berridge, "Britain, South African and African Defence, 1949-55," in *British Foreign Policy, 1945-56*, ed. Michael Dockrill and John W. Young (New York: St. Martin's Press, 1989), 104.

[185]Blaxland, "The Korean War: Reflections on Shared Australian and Canadian Military Experiences," 27.

[186]Glenn St John Barclay, *Friends in High Places: Australian-American Diplomatic Relations since 1945* (Melbourne: Oxford University Press, 1985), 45.

[187]Albert Palazzo, *The Australian Army: A History of its Organisation* (Melbourne: Oxford University Press, 2001), 218.

reasons explain this difference. First, Truman's administration likely believed that Australia's limitations were legitimate. Acheson, for example, offered to provide Australia's government with an aid package to develop its infrastructure without an Australian request for such an offer.[188] Acheson's offer, therefore, supports this possibility.

Second, it is rational to consider that Menzies' government received less "forceful" language than its Commonwealth counterparts did because Truman's administration identified greater commonality with Australia and its government. Neither Truman nor Acheson mentioned this consideration in their memoirs. However, the United States and Australia shared several security concerns in the Pacific. It is possible that Truman's administration saw Australia as a potential bulwark in that region and, thus, wanted to ensure good relations with it.

Australian Prime Minister Robert Menzies fretted about the effects of his nation's legislative restrictions on his government's ability to commit forces to Korea. However, government leaders such as Sir Percy Spender, Minister for External Affairs and External Territories in 1950, knew that Australia had to find a way to contribute forces to Korea. Spender, seeking a Pacific security pact with the United States, understood that Australian forces in Korea enhanced prospects for this pact, and he thus forced Menzies to act.

---

[188]Memorandum of Conversation: Korea; Migration Program; Requirement for Funds, between Dean Acheson and Robert Menzies, July 31, 1950, Papers of Dean Acheson, Harry S. Truman Library, Independence, MO.

Menzies announced that Australia would contribute forces to Korea one hour before Attlee's government announced similar intentions.[189] His timing was significant for two reasons. First, Menzies' announcement prompted the British to rush forces from the garrison in Hong Kong to Korea.[190] This event, though it led to British forces arriving in Korea before Australian forces, provided additional multinational land forces to the UN Command. Therefore, Menzies' announcement helped American ground forces on the Korean peninsula while legitimizing UN credibility. Second, Menzies' timing showed immediate solidarity with the Truman administration. However, Menzies could not immediately contribute Australian forces to the UN Command.

The Australian Army "was not permitted to oblige regular servicemen to serve outside Australia."[191] Troops had to volunteer for overseas service. Menzies' government, for example, could not order Australian troops to serve on occupation duty in Japan. Thus, Australian soldiers serving occupation duty in Japan were all volunteers. Furthermore, Australians were required to be at least 22 years of age to volunteer for overseas service.[192]

Menzies demonstrated Australian credibility and reliability to Truman's administration in two other ways. First, he pursued legislative action to increase the size

---

[189]Grey, *The Commonwealth Armies and the Korean War*, 35.

[190]Ibid., 57.

[191]O'Neill, *Australia in the Korean War 1950-53, Volume I: Strategy and Diplomacy*, 33.

[192]Grey, *The Commonwealth Armies and the Korean War*, 36.

of the Australian Army to 29,104.[193] He announced Australian contributions to Korea, for example, specifically to encourage his government to remove its legislative restrictions on military service.[194] Second, Menzies cancelled plans to remove Australian occupation forces from Japan.[195]

Menzies' actions clearly demonstrated his desire for his nation to play its part "in the defense of the free world"[196] despite its limitations. His actions represented his goal to contribute significantly to operations in Korea. This is significant when one considers that St Laurent's government required substantial prodding from American officials to provide military forces. Additionally, his decision to maintain Australian troops in Japan revealed his willingness to meet Australia's obligations to international security. This decision is significant when one considers Canada's inability to meet a task obligated by the North Atlantic Treaty. Importantly, Menzies' demonstrations of Australian credibility and reliability occurred at a time when Truman felt his nation was "receiving little direct support from allies."[197]

---

[193]Blaxland, "The Korean War: Reflections on Shared Australian and Canadian Military Experiences," 27.

[194]Ibid., 26.

[195]U.S. Department of State, *U.S. Policy in the Korean Crisis* (Washington, DC: Government Printing Office, 1950), 33.

[196]Memorandum of Conversation: Aid to Korea, Truman, Menzies, Acheson, July 28, 1950, Papers of Dean Acheson, Harry S. Truman Library, Independence, MO.

[197]O'Neill, *Australia in the Korean War 1950-53, Volume I: Strategy and Diplomacy*, 111.

One Australian destroyer, one frigate, and a Royal Australian Air Force squadron were operational in Korea by September 1, 1950.[198] Additionally, Australia had another destroyer en route to Korea and was already forming two battalions of infantry. One infantry battalion was operating in Korea by October 6, 1950.[199]

Australian's timeline was very quick if one considers its manpower and deployment restrictions. Furthermore, Australia's timeline far surpassed Canada's pace. Australia's "prompt assistance"[200] received Acheson's expressions of the American State Department's pleasure and thanks. Menzies' desire for a Pacific security agreement with the United States motivated his government to seek measures that negated its national restrictions and supported its participation in Korea.

Menzies' actions increased his nation's chances for an American-Australian security pact in the Pacific. Acheson's expressions of gratitude for Australian assistance reflected the Truman administration's developing awareness of Australia's contributions. American recognition of Australian assistance, thus, increased the Truman administration's likelihood to agree to a Pacific security agreement. The signing of an American-Australian security pact in 1952 confirms this conclusion.

Australian air and naval forces arrived nearly in conjunction with British and Canadian air and naval forces. Australia's ground force was smaller than were its Canadian counterpart. However, this critical resource arrived just over one month after

---

[198]Status of United Nations Military Assistance Offers, September 1, 1950, 1.

[199]Status of United Nations Military Assistance Offers, October 6, 1950, 1.

[200]Memorandum of Conversation: Military Support for Southern Korea, June 29, 1950, Papers of Dean Acheson, Harry S. Truman Library, Independence, MO.

British forces and five weeks prior to Canadian forces.[201] Australia's rapid mobilization and deployment reflected a political desire to show solidarity with the Truman administration. Furthermore, Australian forces aided this cause almost immediately by distinguishing themselves in combat.

Australian forces distinguished themselves in three ways. First, the Royal Australian Air Force's 77th Squadron was the first British Commonwealth unit to see combat in Korea, and the first Commonwealth organization to sustain casualties.[202] Third, ROK President Rhee praised the effects of Australian airpower on the DPRK Army.[203]

Australian forces distinguished themselves in three critical areas. First, Australia immediately provided available forces. This fact reduced pressure on the Truman administration to bear the entire burden in Korea. Second, by not retreating or withdrawing forces after sustaining the first British Commonwealth casualty, Menzies' government sustained the Truman administration's perception of Australian reliability and credibility. Third, Rhee's written recognition of forces from a nation other than the United States is incredibly significant. Rhee's gratitude for Australian military capabilities likely enhanced Australia's credibility throughout the UN and, specifically, with Truman's administration.

---

[201]Barclay, *Friends in High Places: Australian-American Diplomatic Relations since 1945*, 45.

[202]George Odgers, *Across the Parallel: The Australian 77th Squadron with the United States Air Force in the Korean War* (Melbourne: William Heinemann, 1953), 28.

[203]Rhee Syngman, letter to Harry S. Truman, July 17, 1950, President's Secretary's Files, 2. Harry S. Truman Library, Independence, MO.

Truman's administration pursued Australian contributions with tactics that diverged from its discussions with British and Canadian officials. It is conceivable to argue that American perceptions of Australia's limitations created this difference. Regardless, Menzies' government announced swiftly its intentions to support operations in Korea. Australia's rapid mobilization and deployment of forces to Korea validated Menzies' intentions. One may conclude that Australia's haste to reduce its limitations and support Korean operations increased American perceptions of Australian credibility and reliability. Therefore, rapid Australian actions likely prevented Truman's administration from requesting forcefully immediate Australian contributions.

The North Atlantic Treaty obligated the United States to support allies in Western Europe, such as Great Britain, in the event of war with the Soviet Union. Conversely, Australia was not an American ally in June 1950, but merely a potential coalition partner. A treaty did not exist between the United States and Australia that obligated either to support the other's national defense. The Truman administration's reduced patience and poor knowledge with Great Britain and Canada reflected American expectations of immediate contributions from those nations because of pre-existing alliances. Therefore, it is possible that Truman's administration applied different expectations to Australia than it did to Great Britain or Canada. Equally, one may conclude that Truman's administration was simply grateful for any Australian assistance.

Australian contributions, battlefield performance, and an American reassessment of its security interests after June 25, 1950 persuaded the Truman administration to negotiate a security pact with Australia. The United States Senate ratified the security agreement in 1952. It did not contain NATO characteristics such as dedicated staffs, troops, or automatic commitments "in times of crisis.[204] However, the Australia, New Zealand, United States Security Treaty (ANZUS) gave Menzies' government what it sought since the Second World War. Additionally, ANZUS negated Australia's former security reliance on Great Britain and, thus, provided Australia with greater independence within the British Commonwealth. ANZUS also heightened Australia's status to a near-equal diplomatic position with the United States in relation to Great Britain. Politically, the actions of Menzies' government in Korea delivered its desired results.

Logic guided Truman's intent for operations in Korea. He did not want a general war with the Soviet Union or China. Truman's intent, based on realistic expectations, appears to have encouraged nations such as Britain and Canada to contribute military forces to a coalition in Korea. Conversely, emotions provoked by American majorities in men and materiél and American assistance to its allies between 1945 and 1950 appeared to guide American efforts to develop that coalition. Thus, American officials demonstrated that they expected contributions from traditional allies such as Britain and Canada and acted forcefully when those nations professed their inabilities to meet American demands.

The Australian government presented itself as a reliable American partner that did not need encouragement to contribute forces. The Truman administration's conduct gained coalition contributions from Britain and Canada; however, these contributions occurred at significant expense to overall diplomatic relations with these nations. Eventually, considerations such as crossing the 38th Parallel, China's intervention in the

---

[204]Alan Watt, *The Evolution of Australian Foreign Policy 1938-1965* (Cambridge: Cambridge University Press, 1967), 120-121.

war, and Douglas MacArthur's influence increased the tension created by the Truman

administration's efforts to develop a coalition with its Commonwealth partners.

CHAPTER 3

COALITION SUSTAINMENT PART I

Inchon, Crossing the 38th Parallel,
China, and MacArthur

In war, indeed, there can be no substitute for victory.
— Douglas MacArthur, *Reminiscences*

President Harry S. Truman's administration, having built a coalition for Korea,

now needed to sustain that *ad hoc* organization. Sustaining a coalition is more critical

than developing a coalition. Three series of events shaped operations in Korea following

Commonwealth decisions to contribute forces to combat operations. The UN landings at

Inchon and subsequent drive to and beyond the 38th Parallel represent the first series of

events. China's entrance into the Korean War constitutes the second series of events.

Harry Truman's subsequent dismissal of General Douglas MacArthur represents the third

series of events. Identified episodes increased dissension between Truman's

administration and its coalition partners.

The Inchon landings occurred on September 15, 1950.[205] UN forces quickly

gained the strategic advantage following the landings. Political considerations that

required swift decisions rapidly arose. The subsequent UN offensive brought American-

led forces closer to the border at the 38th Parallel between North and South Korea. The

UN operations that continued across the 38th Parallel increased the risk of a wider war

---

[205]U.S. Department of State, Foreign Policy Studies Branch, Chronology of
Principle Events Relating to the Korean Conflict, September 1950, 10.

because they were likely to encourage Soviet or Chinese intervention. Chinese forces entered Korea in late October 1950.

Chinese intervention was avoidable before October 1950. The original UN mandate resolved to defend the ROK's sovereignty. The UN Command's strategic objective sought to control militarily South Korean territory. Controlling ROK territory created conditions that prevented North Korean forces from operating in that territory. Reaching the 38th Parallel ensured the defeat of North Korea's military. Therefore, the UN Command accomplished the UN objective by reaching the 38th Parallel. This does not insinuate that China would not have eventually invaded Korea to restore a friendly government on its border. However, China likely would not have sent military forces into Korea had the UN Command remained at the 38th Parallel, specifically if the UN Command retained its troops in South Korea to develop the ROK army and establish a formidable defensive line near the 38th Parallel.

Commonwealth nations contributed forces to the American-led coalition in Korea to protect the ROK's sovereignty. Great Britain, Canada, and Australia did not join the UN Command to unify all of Korea under one government. They wanted to accomplish the UN mandate and legitimize the UN organization. Therefore, Truman, changing the strategic objective by seeking to unify the Korean Peninsula, unnecessarily created conditions that reduced his administration's ability to sustain the coalition it laboriously built.

By July 12, 1950, the Truman administration remained undecided regarding the UN's military courses of action "after the North Koreans have been driven" across the

38th Parallel.[206] Truman's Administrative Assistant wrote the memorandum containing this quote nearly two months before the Inchon landings. Thus, Truman's assistant wrote this memo while American land forces maintained a perilous situation in Korea. The UN Command remained incapable of protecting the ROK's sovereignty at that time.

American indecision provides two considerations. First, it exhibited an American assumption that the UN Command would eventually drive the DPRK Army back across the 38th Parallel. Truman's assumption, therefore, reflected either his total confidence in the UN Command's ultimate success or a racist attitude against the DPRK. It is certainly wise for strategists and decision-makers to ponder future operations. To ignore future contingencies is irresponsible leadership. However, political and military leaders cannot afford to assume success, as Truman's assistant's memo suggests, if their forces are at risk for expulsion from the battleground. The EUSA faced this situation in July 1950.

The second consideration Truman's indecision portrays is his failure to consider coalition partner thoughts and concerns regarding his decision. Truman cannot receive fault completely for this failure. The United States contributed the majority of land forces to Korea. The Truman administration's position of leadership in Korea provided it with sole responsibility for the war's outcome. Thus, one can reasonably conclude that Truman identified multinational contributions, such as Britain's two battalions, as insufficient to warrant those nations' wishes to influence his administration's decisions.

---

[206]Memo from George M. Elsey to the National Security Council, July 12, 1950, Papers of George M. Elsey, Harry S. Truman Library, Independence, MO.

Truman's administration received "primary responsibility"[207] to lead operations in Korea from the UN. However, the British and Australian governments had already announced intentions to send military forces to Korea by July 12, 1950. Great Britain and Australia became members of the UN Command by way of their military contributions. Therefore, Truman's administration should have included immediately its Commonwealth partners' opinions once it began pondering the decision to cross the 38th Parallel. Inclusion of this sort would ensure that American decision-making considered the concerns of nations that contributed forces. Furthermore, inclusion of other nations' considerations would confirm that those nations possessed sufficient political will and domestic support to continue contributing forces to operations in Korea, even if the military situation changed.

Truman's administration did receive British input on the decision to cross the 38th Parallel in late July 1950. The participants in these meetings determined that responsibility for operations beyond the 38th Parallel rested with the UN.[208] However, Commonwealth members such as Canada wanted assurance that operations in Korea were not "merely an endorsement by the United Nations of unilateral action by the United States."[209] Specifically, these nations wanted to ensure that Truman's decisions created conditions that supported the coalition's ability to accomplish the UN mission.

---

[207]U.S. Department of State, World Reaction to Korean Developments, Special Supplement, July 18, 1950, Harry S. Truman Library, Independence, MO.

[208]U.S. Department of State, "Memorandum of Conversation, U.S.-U.K. Discussions on Present World Situation, 20-24 July 1950, General Omar Bradley, Ambassador Phillip C. Jessup and Sir Oliver Franks, Lord Tedder," Harry S. Truman Library, Independence, MO.

[209]Melady, *Korea: Canada's Forgotten War*, 28.

Thus, Commonwealth governments did not want Truman's administration to pursue courses of action likely to serve purely American interests and risked escalating the war.

Louis St Laurent, Canada's Prime Minister, correctly pursued such assurances. Commonwealth nations contributed military forces to the UN Command to restore the ROK government. Commonwealth populations supported this cause. The potential for Truman's administration to act unilaterally in Korea risked the goal for which Commonwealth leaders contributed forces to Korea. Extending operations beyond the 38th Parallel risked a wider war with China or the Soviet Union. Furthermore, Commonwealth political leaders could not guarantee that their constituents would support a UN advance into the DPRK.

A resolution sanctioned by the UN determined that defending the ROK was a vital interest to global stability. In the Korean War example, crossing the 38th Parallel meant changing the UN's objective. Changing a coalition objective, or considering changing it, is problematic. A change of objectives is likely to reduce coalition unity. Additionally, changing the objective lessens the potential for non-participating nations to contribute forces. Furthermore, changing objectives is likely to reduce the willingness of current contributors to continue providing military forces for purposes beyond the initial objective.

The United States Joint Chiefs of Staff (JCS) felt that crossing the 38th Parallel was legally consistent with the UN mission to "restore peace and unity to Korea."[210] The JCS used its perception of the resolution to justify its recommendation to allow UN forces to invade the DPRK. Therefore, Truman authorized Secretary of Defense George

---

[210]Pogue, *George C. Marshall, Statesman, 1945-1959*, 455.

C. Marshall to advise MacArthur that he should "feel unhampered tactically and strategically to proceed north of the 38th Parallel."[211] MacArthur willingly followed his commander-in-chief's order.

The JCS recommendation is sensible from a military perspective. The DPRK government's existence posed a permanent threat to peace on the Korean peninsula. Thus, destroying the DPRK's army reduced the risks the DPRK presented to Korean and global stability. Furthermore, the UN Command maintained the military advantage and appeared capable of destroying the DPRK army. Additionally, denying the UN Command authority to cross the 38th Parallel prevented any hope of unifying Korea according to the UN resolution.

The JCS ignored the political consequences of its recommendation. It is conceivable that the Commonwealth governments did not share the Joint Chief's interpretation of the UN's resolution. Therefore, the JCS recommendation ignored the likely Commonwealth perspective that restoring peace to Korea meant merely the restoration of the ROK government. America's senior military leaders forgot that they represented a nation that was one of many conducting operations in Korea.

Truman's administration could not depend on the Commonwealth to follow blindly American policies. The UN Command was going to face difficulty in northern Korea, with or without Chinese interference, due to the region's restrictive terrain and winter weather. Eventually, Commonwealth war weariness would increase through these military difficulties and force Commonwealth governments to reconsider their

---

[211]Ibid., 457.

80

contributions. Thus, the JCS recommendation created potential for American forces to find themselves fighting in Korea with only ROK forces.

Truman's decision to cross the 38th Parallel created two problems. Rhee Syngman, the ROK President, represented Truman's first concern. Truman's second difficulty centered on the imprecise guidance he provided to MacArthur. Truman's guidance was vulnerable to MacArthur's misinterpretation and, therefore, made difficult Truman's ability to sustain the UN coalition after its military forces crossed the 38th Parallel.

Rhee's government had a poor reputation internationally prior to June 25, 1950. Clement Attlee's government, for example, identified the ROK as a "totalitarian police state" for Rhee's indifference to constitutional processes.[212] Regardless, Rhee wanted to unify all of Korea under his control. The ROK President's goal, thus, turned him into an even more difficult ally for Truman and the Commonwealth governments. Rhee, for example, personally rejected peace proposals from the DPRK after the Inchon landings to accomplish his goal to unify the Korean peninsula.[213]

Rhee did not consult with his coalition partners when he rejected North Korean peace proposals. Two reasons justify his actions. First, Kim Il-Sung, North Korea's Prime Minster, shared Rhee's goal to unify Korea under his "respective terms."[214] Therefore, it is likely to conclude that North Korea's proposals were merely ploys to buy time to

---

[212]Stebbins, *The United States in World Affairs, 1950*, 186.

[213]U.S. Department of State, Foreign Policy Studies Branch, Chronology of Principle Events Relating to the Korean Conflict, September 1950, 13.

[214]Gaddis, *We Now Know: Rethinking Cold War History*, 71.

reconstitute its military forces and resume operations to unify Korea under a communist government.

Second, the ROK elected Rhee democratically to serve as its first President. Rhee's election occurred under UN sponsorship. Sanctioned democratic elections enabled Rhee to operate from a credible position of power. Therefore, Rhee's situation permitted him to choose political and military courses of action, independent of wishes from Truman, the Commonwealth governments, or the UN Command, to satisfy South Korea's national interests. Rhee's actions likely affected Truman's decision to cross the 38th Parallel. However, his conduct increased tension between the UN Command's participating governments.

The UN resolved to defend the ROK from aggression and restore the Rhee government to power. Members of the UN overwhelmingly voted in support of the organization's resolution. However, it is reasonable to accept that members of the UN favored the resolution regardless of their perceptions of Rhee's regime. Furthermore, it is feasible to believe that nations that disliked Rhee's practices contributed forces to the UN Command to enhance UN credibility. Therefore, it is conceivable to conclude that nations such as Great Britain did not contribute forces to Korea simply to protect Rhee's personal leadership. Conversely, it is also logical to conclude that UN members supported Rhee simply because he was anti-communist.

Rhee, however, did not have authority to gain political control of Korea north of the 38th Parallel through military force. UN sponsored elections did not occur in that region. Moreover, Commonwealth governments, specifically Attlee's, were unwilling to support Rhee's leadership of northern Korea without peninsula-wide elections.[215] Thus, Rhee's rejection of DPRK peace proposals risked alienating the coalition that supported him. However, Rhee possessed one significant advantage against the Commonwealth's perceptions of his harsh style of government.

Politically, Truman could not abandon Rhee. Rhee was an American ally. Truman, by deserting Rhee in war, would reduce American credibility in the eyes of nations that depended on American support. Furthermore, forsaking Rhee in war would cause nations dependent on American assistance to lose trust in the United States in times of peace. Additionally, an American desertion of an ally against a communist threat would likely encourage additional communist uprisings around the world. Therefore, Truman probably did not decide independently to cross the 38th Parallel to achieve American aims. Rhee's effect on Truman's decision appears obvious. Unfortunately, Rhee's determination to unify Korea created conditions that resulted in China's military intervention.

Truman never stopped hoping to prevent Chinese involvement in Korea. To negate China's potential interference in Korea, Truman initially ordered MacArthur to cross the 38th Parallel with only ROK forces.[216] Therefore, Truman could claim that ROK forces were attempting independently to achieve Korean aims and unify their

---

[215]Fitzsimmons, *The Foreign Policy of the British Labour Government 1945-1951*, 137.

[216]Jack Gallaway, *The Last Call of the Bugle: The Long Road to Kapyong* (Queensland: University of Queensland Press, 1999), 59.

peninsula. ROK forces crossed the 38th Parallel on October 1, 1950.[217] However, Truman soon authorized MacArthur to use non-Korean forces to enter the DPRK and advance north under three stipulations.

First, Truman allowed MacArthur to continue advancing beyond the 38th Parallel so long as MacArthur felt that operations presented "a reasonable chance of success."[218] Second, operations were to cease immediately if "imminent danger"[219] of Soviet or Chinese intervention arose. Third, Truman denied MacArthur permission to deploy non-Korean forces near Korea's immediate borders with the Soviet Union and China.[220] From an American perspective, Truman did everything conceivably possible to prevent China from entering the war.

However, Truman's efforts to restrict MacArthur ignored reality in three areas. First, Truman's restrictions contrasted with Marshall's initial instructions that allowed MacArthur to feel "unhampered" as the UN Command crossed the 38th Parallel. Truman's subsequent restrictions to his initial guidance could confuse any military commander's understanding of their commander-in-chief's true intent. However, MacArthur was not a typical military commander. MacArthur was a commander likely to remain content to operate with the guidance provided in Marshall's note. Unfortunately,

---

[217]U.S. Department of State, Foreign Policy Studies Branch, Chronology of Principle Events Relating to the Korean Conflict, October 1950, i.

[218]Truman, *Memoirs by Harry S. Truman, Volume II: Years of Trial and Hope*, 383.

[219]Johnston, *A War of Patrols: Canadian Army Operations in Korea*, 36.

[220]Denis Stairs, *The Diplomacy of Constraint: Canada, the Korean War, and the United States* (Toronto: University of Toronto Press, 1974), 133.

no one could truly stop MacArthur from operating according to his personal whims and desires once non-Korean forces crossed the 38th Parallel.

Second, Truman's subsequent guidance to continue operations that offered "reasonable" chances for success was not sufficiently restrictive. Therefore, Truman's guidance allowed MacArthur to interpret orders as he preferred. MacArthur's reputation as a self-serving commander makes concerning Truman's guidance regarding "reasonable" success. Truman, a politician seeking to maintain a coalition and domestic American support for the war in Korea, was likely to define "reasonable" in one manner. Conversely, MacArthur, with vast experience as a military commander, was likely to define "reasonable" in a manner different from Truman.

Third, Truman's restrictions ignored China's obvious warnings. Zhou Enlai, China's Premier, called the United States China's "most dangerous enemy" in September 1950.[221] Zhou's intention to protect the DPRK is unmistakable with hindsight. However, Zhou's warnings to the UN Command clearly exhibited in 1950 the "imminent danger" Truman wanted to avoid after authorizing MacArthur to cross the 38th Parallel. Additionally, crossing the 38th Parallel with non-ROK military forces supported communist claims that the United States was the war's aggressor. Unfortunately, Truman and the UN Command ignored Zhou's warnings.

Three possible reasons exist to explain the West's ignorance regarding Zhou's warnings. First, Truman possibly maintained total confidence in MacArthur's decision-making. Truman appointed MacArthur to command all UN forces. MacArthur's

---

[221]U.S. Department of State, Foreign Policy Studies Branch, Chronology of Principle Events Relating to the Korean Conflict, September 1950, 30.

appointment infers Truman's trust in the general's leadership. This inference represents any time a commander-in-chief appoints someone to a command position. However, Truman believed that MacArthur "wasn't right in his head."[222] Truman's perception, therefore, rejects this first possible reason for the West's ignorance of Chinese intentions.

Second, Truman's administration faced substantial criticism from Republicans in the United States Congress for perceptions of the administration's lack of toughness against communism. The Congress, for example, charged Truman's administration with responsibility for the "Communist victory" in China in 1949.[223] Additionally, American politicians continuously called throughout the Korean War for Truman to fire his Secretary of State, Dean Acheson, for incompetence and softness against communism.[224] Therefore, it is reasonable to conclude that intense domestic pressure within the United States preempted Truman's inclination to prevent non-ROK forces from crossing the 38th Parallel.

Third, UN multinational forces achieved rapid success against the DPRK's army after the Inchon landings in September 1950. Therefore, it is reasonable to conclude that Truman's administration and its Commonwealth counterparts perceived the Chinese army as just slightly more capable militarily than North Korea. One can reasonably identify China's numerical superiority and, possibly, its relationship with the Soviet Union as the Truman administration's primary concerns regarding Chinese intervention

---

[222]Miller, *Plain Speaking: An Oral Biography of Harry S. Truman*, 291.

[223]Truman, *Memoirs by Harry S. Truman, Volume II: Years of Trial and Hope*, 430.

[224]Ibid., 428-431.

in Korea. Truman's administration likely perceived American firepower as capable of negating China's numerical superiority. Moreover, restricting the UN Command's access to the Soviet-Korean border and relying on the Soviets to maintain a Europe-first strategy could prevent the appearance of Soviet forces on the Korean battlefield. Thus, it is logical to conclude that Truman's administration felt that crossing the 38th Parallel was justified under these conditions. However, Truman ignored a critical obligation.

Coalition leaders own the responsibility to maintain unity of effort until the coalition's mission is complete. Truman was the coalition's political leader. He received this authority from the UN Security Council.[225] Therefore, Truman retains primary responsibility for the decision to allow non-ROK forces to cross the 38th Parallel. However, Truman's decision appeared to disregard his obligation to maintain unity of effort with the Commonwealth governments and within the UN Command.

Domestic charges of his administration's weakness likely affected Truman's decision. However, it is rational to believe that Truman did not make decisions from an American-only perspective. Rhee's ultimate goals likely played as significant a role as domestic considerations in Truman's decision-making process. Evidence, demonstrated through Truman's guidance to MacArthur, suggests that Truman accounted for Commonwealth concerns regarding Chinese intervention but ignored them to satisfy Rhee. Regardless, Truman's decision to cross the 38th Parallel enhanced the likelihood of a "new war"[226] that he wanted to prevent.

---

[225] Statement by the President, July 8, 1950, Papers of George M. Elsey, Harry S. Truman Library, Independence, MO.

[226] MacArthur, *Reminiscences*, 368.

Truman's well-intentioned guidance ignored credible Chinese threats. Additionally, his guidance was sufficiently vulnerable to MacArthur misinterpretations and, thus, likely to provoke Chinese involvement. Furthermore, Truman's coalition, created through substantial effort, was unprepared for and in some cases unwilling to participate in this new war. Truman's decision to extend the war, therefore, increased friction in a coalition that his administration built under strenuous effort. Tension with Truman's decision was evident within the British Commonwealth nations that contributed forces to Korea.

Attlee's government noted three primary concerns with crossing the 38th Parallel and invading the DPRK with non-ROK forces. First, Attlee's government, in contrast to the United States JCS, doubted the legality of crossing the 38th Parallel.[227] Specifically, the original UN resolution resolved to repel the DPRK attack. The resolution did not support Korean unification through military force.

Negative effects on coalition unity represent the second Attlee government concern regarding operations into the DPRK. Specifically, Attlee wanted Truman to ensure that all decisions were capable of maintaining the UN's "impressive degree of unanimity over Korea."[228] Attlee's government understood that the UN, minus dissension from nations in the Soviet bloc, supported the defense of the ROK. Attlee did not want to disrupt that unity. He correctly interpreted the risks inherent in crossing the 38th Parallel.

---

[227]U.S. Department of State, *Foreign Relations of the United States 1950*, vol. 3, 1157.

[228]Farrar-Hockley, *The British Part in the Korean War, Volume I: A Distant Obligation*, 191.

UN resolutions for Operation Desert Shield/Desert Storm parallel the British government's concern for crossing the 38th Parallel. Specifically, the UN resolved to conduct Desert Shield/Desert Storm to repel Saddam Hussein's Iraqi Army from Kuwait. This commitment did not include a mandate to remove Hussein from power. United States President George H.W. Bush wisely followed the legal spirit and letter of the UN resolution. Bush's decision preserved his coalition's unity and prevented possibilities for a wider war in the Middle East. The same example, with a different result, occurred in Korea.

Attlee's third concern revolved around the effect of Soviet or Chinese involvement on UN unity. An invasion by either country would expand the war and, thus, reverse the Attlee-Truman goal of keeping the war localized to Korea. Attlee initially felt that the new Communist Chinese government was a Soviet satellite state. He perceived that the Soviet Union would identify UN operations north of the 38th Parallel as a UN effort to remove the new Chinese government.[229] Attlee, thus, felt the Soviets would intervene in Korea to deter the UN advance across the 38th Parallel from planning to invade China. Attlee's hopes to maintain the coalition's unity motivated his concern. However, British interests also inspired Attlee to seek all means possible to keep China out of the Korean War.

Attlee wanted his nation to maintain "the friendliest possible relationship" with whatever was the government of China at any given moment.[230] Attlee's government

---

[229]Ibid., 193.

[230]Fitzsimmons, *The Foreign Policy of the British Labour Government 1945-1951*, 133.

recognized China's communist government in January 1950.[231] British leaders pursued

this diplomatic path to ensure protection for British commercial interests in China after

the Communist government assumed control.[232] Chinese belligerency in Korea posed risk

to British commercial interests in China. Therefore, Attlee took China's warnings

literally and correctly assumed that crossing the 38th Parallel would invite Chinese

intervention and thereby expand the war.

Attlee cannot receive blame for seeking to protect his nation's interests. He

supported Truman's decision despite his concerns for Britain's welfare. However,

coalitions typically conduct operations for the greater welfare of the world. Coalitions do

not conduct operations specifically for the benefit of one nation. A free and independent

Republic of Korea served the West's collective interests. Attlee's concerns represented a

significant separation between American and British goals in Korea, and the means these

nations sought to achieve those goals. This divide existed throughout the remainder of the

Korean War. A similar concern arose between the United States and Canada.

Canada's St Laurent government found itself unwelcome to participate in the

Truman administration's deliberations on crossing the 38th Parallel. Canada's air forces

were transporting United States troops to Korea. Canadian naval vessels participated in

the Inchon landings.[233] It is conceivable to assume that St Laurent's government was

---

[231]Dockrill, "The Foreign Office, Anglo-American Relations and the Korean War, June 1950-June 1951," 459.

[232]Fitzsimmons, *The Foreign Policy of the British Labour Government 1945-1951*, 134.

[233]Blaxland, "The Korean War: Reflections on Shared Australian and Canadian Military Experiences," 28.

providing all resources possible within its constraints. Regardless, Canada's promised

ground forces had yet to reach Korea when Truman made his decision. Therefore,

Truman's administration appeared to disregard Canadian opinions in its deliberations on

crossing the 38th Parallel.

American officials such as Acheson complained about Canada's inability to

provide "significant forces"[234] to Korea. However, this complaint ignored the fact that

Canada was contributing to the UN Command. American ignorance in this example is

problematic. It supports the argument that Truman's administration determined a

coalition partner's ability to influence or participate in planning and decision-making

according to the size, type, and timing of that nation's contributions. Therefore, American

ignorance to Canadian contributions created tension with a permanent United States ally.

American ignorance to Canadian contributions did not stop St Laurent's

government from declaring its thoughts publicly to the UN General Assembly and

"confidentially"[235] to the Truman Administration. St Laurent's perspective of post-

Inchon operations represents two critical points. First, the Canadian approach to Korea

appeared to complement British objectives of limiting the war to the accomplishment of

the original UN mandate. Second, Canada did not share the American objective to unify

the Korean peninsula. American-Canadian differences on the future of Korea put

Canada's military forces into a situation for which they did not expect. However, St

Laurent's government did not follow the American lead with Attlee's level of acceptance.

---

[234]Johnston, *A War of Patrols: Canadian Army Operations in Korea*, 37.

[235]Stairs, *The Diplomacy of Constraint: Canada, the Korean War, and the United States*, 132.

St Laurent's government shared four mutual perspectives with the British. First, Canadian leaders shared the Attlee government's perspective on the legality of crossing the 38th Parallel. Therefore, St Laurent's government argued for a cautious approach to extending the UN's mandate in Korea.[236] Furthermore, Britain and Canada shared a goal to create a buffer zone between Korea and China. A buffer zone could limit the war and thereby reduce the likelihood of Chinese or Soviet intervention after UN forces crossed the 38th Parallel.[237] Third, both nations suggested that the DPRK receive an opportunity to agree to a cease-fire.[238] Fourth, both nations protested the attention Truman's administration paid to Korea at the expense of their top security priority, Europe.[239]

Truman never opposed the premise that Europe was his primary security interest. Nonetheless, he likely understood that the situation in Korea needed to be resolved for European security to receive his full attention and military support. Following Inchon, St Laurent protested that Canada's obligation to Korea ended with the "restoration of peace and the defeat of aggression in Korea."[240] However, the UN objective for Korea changed on October 7, 1950. The UN approved a new mandate that resolved to create a "unified,

---

[236]Melady, *Korea: Canada's Forgotten War*, 60.

[237]Stairs, *The Diplomacy of Constraint: Canada, the Korean War, and the United States*, 132.

[238]Melady, *Korea: Canada's Forgotten War*, 60-61.

[239]Stairs, *The Diplomacy of Constraint: Canada, the Korean War, and the United States*, 149.

[240]Ibid., 116.

independent, and democratic" Korean government.[241] Thus, the situation in Korea could only conclude through Korean unification.

St Laurent's quote regarding the "restoration of peace" reflected his clear support for the original UN mandate. However, his quote regarding the "defeat of aggression" is vague. It did not clearly define his position. "Defeating aggression" could simply refer to St Laurent's support for repelling the DPRK military from South Korea. Conversely, "defeating aggression" could imply that St Laurent wanted to remove communist influence from Korea to prevent another DPRK invasion of the ROK. Given his previous speeches, it is reasonable to conclude that St Laurent's statement implied his unwillingness to provide Canadian ground forces in support of Korean unification. This implication, therefore, indicated that substantial differences existed between the Canada and the United States.

Rhee also contributed to these differences. The ROK President argued that stopping at the 38th Parallel after the Inchon landings was unacceptable to Koreans. His statement placed Truman in a significant predicament. Truman's unwillingness or inability to support his ally would reduce America's international credibility as a deterrent to communist aggression. Robert Menzies' government, on the other hand, presented an appearance of enthusiastic compliance with the new UN mandate and the Truman administration's goals.

After the Inchon landings, Menzies' government, compared to other British Commonwealth partners, presented its nation as the Truman administration's most

---

[241]Fitzsimmons, *The Foreign Policy of the British Labour Government 1945-1951*, 136.

trustworthy coalition partner. Menzies, like his fellow Commonwealth leaders, feared an

escalation of the war with the Soviet Union.[242] However, he appeared to share Truman's

understanding of the effects that operations in Korea had on the international community.

Specifically, Menzies seemed to understand that failing to support an ally and accomplish

UN mandates would negatively affect UN credibility and encourage future communist

aggression.

Australian commercial interests and military limitations do not appear to have

affected Menzies' perspective. Three political reasons prompted Menzies to recommend

crossing the 38th Parallel to defeat the DPRK Army. First, he wanted to maintain the

positive relations his government developed with Truman's administration in the early

months of the war. Second, he understood that failing to defeat the DPRK Army by not

crossing the 38th Parallel "would merely mean that we should have another aggression

the next day."[243] Third, he knew that North Korean aggression against South Korea "was

a signal to encourage Communist risings throughout Asia."[244]

Clearly, Menzies understood that North Korea's army would remain capable of

future aggression against the ROK if it were not decisively defeated. From an Australian

perspective, decisively defeating the DPRK favored Australian security because it would

dissuade potential future communist aggression in Asia. Additionally, North Korea's

probability of acting aggressively against its southern neighbor in the future would force

---

[242]O'Neill, *Australia in the Korean War 1950-53. Volume I: Strategy and Diplomacy*, 130.

[243]Ibid., 122.

[244]Henry S. Albinski, "Australia Faces China," *Asian Survey* 2, no. 2 (April 1962): 17.

the UN to respond with a new series of resolutions. This would inadvertently affect public support within UN member nations for such a situation and indirectly reduce the organization's credibility.

Truman's administration struggled in 1950 to secure contributions from nations such as Canada. American abilities to repeat this effort would find increased difficulty if North Korea conducted another invasion of South Korea. UN members and, specifically, their domestic constituents would wonder why the coalition failed to accomplish its mission the first time and question a coalition's ability to accomplish the new mission. Additionally, an organization's failure to achieve an objective, regardless of its restrictions, reduces that organization's credibility. Therefore, the UN Command needed to defeat North Korea's army.

The United States-led coalition that fought in Operation Desert Shield/Desert Storm did not topple Saddam Hussein's government. UN mandates did not require Hussein's removal. The United States returned to Iraq 12 years later to depose Hussein's government. Criticism for America's inability to "get the job done" the first time was in abundance. Therefore, among other reasons, American leaders faced resistance to their efforts to build a new coalition in 2002-2003. Therefore, failure to defeat decisively North Korea's army when the opportunity presented itself would repeat history in a manner that Menzies found unnecessary.

Militarily, Menzies argued, advancing forces should maintain their initiative and not abandon their advantage after reaching "a certain parallel of latitude."[245] His

---

[245] O'Neill, *Australia in the Korean War 1950-53. Volume I: Strategy and Diplomacy*, 122.

argument made military sense and supported his political perspective. It did not stop Menzies from joining his Commonwealth counterparts to recommend an operational pause at Korea's "narrow waist"[246] to deter Chinese intervention. However, Menzies' primary recommendations exhibited a desire to accomplish a mission, Korean unification, which Truman's administration felt bound to accomplish according to the new UN resolution. Crossing the 38th Parallel produced initial success for the United Nations Command. Unfortunately, it also created several negative conditions that reduced the coalition's unity of effort.

It is worth mentioning a ROK general's identification of Chinese soldiers in Korea by the end of October 1950.[247] This occurred roughly two weeks after non-Korean UN forces crossed the 38th Parallel. UN forces identified China's 124th Division in Korea two days later.[248] Chinese intervention, in opposition to Winston Churchill's claim, was clearly not a simple attempt to divert attention away from Western Europe.[249] It was an invasion designed to remove UN forces from the DPRK and the Korean

---

[246]Stairs, *The Diplomacy of Constraint: Canada, the Korean War, and the United States*, 132.

[247]U.S. Department of State, Foreign Policy Studies Branch, Chronology of Principle Events Relating to the Korean Conflict, October 1950, 33.

[248]U.S. Department of State, Foreign Policy Studies Branch, Chronology of Principle Events Relating to the Korean Conflict, November 1950, ii.

[249]Fitzsimmons, *The Foreign Policy of the British Labour Government 1945-1951*, 137.

peninsula. UN forces initiated a retreat and evacuated Pyongyang, North Korea's capital, on December 4, 1950.[250]

During the war's first several months, Truman did not hide his desire for the war to remain localized to Korea.[251] Primarily, he sought a limited conflict because he knew an escalation of the war would reduce America's capacity to defend Western Europe. Furthermore, unlimited war in Korea would induce Chinese or Soviet participation. This objective explains the logic behind Truman's referring to the war in Korea as a "police action."[252] Truman, thus, continually emphasized his intention to limit operations in Korea to reassure his European allies of America's commitments to their security.

Comments by Truman's advisors forced the Commonwealth governments to question his sincerity. Dean Acheson, for example, claimed that it would be "sheer madness"[253] for the Chinese to enter the war. Acheson's comment dared the Chinese government to enter the war and prove its military mettle. Furthermore, it demonstrated his ignorance to China's warnings.

Acheson reversed his perspective after the Chinese invasion. He admitted that UN forces could not defeat the People's Volunteer Army and unify the Korean peninsula because of China's overwhelming numerical superiority. He recommended that UN

---

[250]U.S. Department of State, Foreign Policy Studies Branch, Chronology of Principle Events Relating to the Korean Conflict, December 1950, ii.

[251]U.S. Department of State, *Foreign Relations of the United States 1950,* vol. 3, 1662.

[252]U.S. Department of State, White House Press and Radio News Conference, President Harry S. Truman, June 29, 1950.

[253]U.S. Department of State, Foreign Policy Studies Branch, Chronology of Principle Events Relating to the Korean Conflict, September 1950, 7-8.

forces "find a line that we can hold, and hold it"[254] soon after China's numerical superiority forced the UN retreats. The UN coalition, thus, found itself unable to retain the military initiative.

The Commonwealth nations felt the blame for this situation rested primarily with MacArthur. Jointly, they claimed he "went beyond"[255] the objectives established by the UN resolution. Canada's Minister for External Affairs, Lester Pearson, urged negotiations with the Chinese government immediately after its invasion.[256] Menzies' government, "rattled"[257] by China's invasion, recognized quickly the dangers Chinese involvement posed to the UN Command's mission in Korea.[258] Attlee's government, motivated to protect British commercial interests in China, reverted to its "original caution" and pursued efforts to keep the war contained to Korea.[259] Truman's administration did not appreciate the Commonwealth's claims, suggestions, or its perceived loss of willpower to accomplish the UN resolution.

---

[254]Memorandum of Conversation: Notes on National Security Council Meeting, November 28, 1950, 5. Papers of Dean Acheson, Harry S. Truman Library, Independence, MO.

[255]U.S. Department of State, Foreign Policy Studies Branch, Chronology of Principle Events Relating to the Korean Conflict, December 1950, 10.

[256]U.S. Department of State, Foreign Policy Studies Branch, Chronology of Principle Events Relating to the Korean Conflict, December 1950, 13.

[257]Richard Trembath, *A Different Sort of War: Australians in Korea, 1950-53* (Melbourne: Australian Scholarly Publishing, 2005), 12.

[258]O'Neill, *Australia in the Korean War 1950-53. Volume I: Strategy and Diplomacy*, 99.

[259]Fitzsimmons, *The Foreign Policy of the British Labour Government 1945-1951*, 137.

Truman and his advisors were also not pleased with MacArthur's inflated projections of a quick victory or his dismissal of Chinese military capabilities. However, they found the timing behind Commonwealth criticism of MacArthur interesting. Specifically, Truman's administration did not identify Commonwealth criticism for American decisions until the Chinese invasion.[260] Therefore, Commonwealth support for American decisions, according to Truman's administration, required successful operations to continue. This American perception created discontent for the Commonwealth within the Truman administration. General Omar Bradley, Chairman of the United States JCS, went so far as to suggest that coalition members should leave the coalition if they were unhappy with American leadership.[261]

American patience for coalition concerns, as demonstrated by Bradley, was nearly negligible. Respect from the Truman administration for coalition contributions was rapidly declining as the United States continued to bear financially and militarily the majority of the war effort. Conversely, British Commonwealth confidence in American leadership was deteriorating. China's negative effects on coalition unity would never have happened if the UN objective to preserve South Korea's government remained consistent. Additionally, coalition dissension and American public support for the war began adversely to affect each other.

---

[260]U.S. Department of State, Foreign Policy Studies Branch, Chronology of Principle Events Relating to the Korean Conflict, November 1950, vi.

[261]Peter Lowe, "The Significance of the Korean War in Anglo-American Relations, 1950-53," in *British Foreign Policy, 1945-56*, ed. Michael Dockrill and John W. Young (New York: St. Martin's Press, 1989), 130.

Eighty-one percent of the American population supported the Korean War in June 1950. Conversely, greater than two-thirds of the American population supported a withdrawal of United States forces from Korea soon after China's invasion.[262] Reduced American popular support for the war started because of MacArthur, who had a distinguished reputation in the United States. The UN commander publicly identified Commonwealth criticism of operations in Korea after China's intervention as a "somewhat selfish though most short-sighted viewpoint."[263]

American citizens already felt their nation bore a greater share than necessary of the burden for Korea. MacArthur made other public comments after the Chinese invasion until his dismissal that demonstrated contempt for his perception of the Commonwealth's unwillingness to unify Korea. Additionally, MacArthur's comments during the United States Congress's investigation of his dismissal increased popular American perceptions that the Commonwealth was not providing sufficient forces to the UN Command.[264] Domestic critics of Truman's administration supported MacArthur's claims against the Commonwealth nations and, thus, further reduced American popular support for the Korean War.

---

[262] Astor, *Presidents at War: From Truman to Bush, the Gathering of Military Power to Our Commanders in Chief*, 41.

[263] U.S. Department of State, Foreign Policy Studies Branch, Chronology of Principle Events Relating to the Korean Conflict, December 1950, 2.

[264] O'Neill, *Australia in the Korean War 1950-53*, 249.

Former President Herbert Hoover, for example, argued in December 1950 that coalition nations were "not doing their share"[265] in Korea. He later affixed blame for the coalition's faltering unity of effort to coalition partners that he identified as appeasers to China.[266] Senator Robert Taft claimed after Chinese intervention that the United States was "sucked" into the Korean War, and soon called for an immediate withdrawal from the Korean peninsula.[267] Senator Richard Nixon publicly complained about America's majority of combat forces in Korea in comparison to its coalition partners' limited contributions.[268]

These statements and their effects on American popular support for the war in Korea exemplify the effect of domestic opinions on a coalition's unity of effort. Unity of effort depends on a shared understanding of the coalition's objectives and an appreciation for multinational contributions regardless of their size. Domestic audiences must understand the coalition's objective as well as the coalition's political and military leaders. Comprehension of this nature, specifically within the lead nation's domestic audience, is likely to ensure that audience's appreciation for multinational military contributions. Therefore, understanding the coalition's mission and its potential struggles

---

[265]U.S. Department of State, Foreign Policy Studies Branch, Chronology of Principle Events Relating to the Korean Conflict, December 1950, iv.

[266]U.S. Department of State, Foreign Policy Studies Branch, Chronology of Principle Events Relating to the Korean Conflict, February 1951, 15.

[267]U.S. Department of State, Foreign Policy Studies Branch, Chronology of Principle Events Relating to the Korean Conflict, January 1951, 9, 11.

[268]Ibid., 54.

is likely to develop a domestic appreciation for the fact that multiple nations share the coalition's burden.

Political leaders possess the responsibility to ensure their audiences understand the coalition mission and, therefore, appreciate multinational contributions. Lester Pearson's suggestion to negotiate with the Chinese immediately after their intervention appeared to validate Hoover's claim that coalition members sought to appease China. However, Pearson wanted to prevent a full-scale war with China. Thus, Pearson shared Truman's goal to limit the war to Korea. Truman's administration retained responsibility to ensure that the American public understood firmly this common objective. The Truman administration failed to do so effectively. Thus, Truman's administration created conditions that permitted statements by political figures to affect negatively American popular support for the war and Commonwealth contributions.

Attlee's government felt that American comments represented a lack of American appreciation for the Commonwealth's contributions and limitations.[269] Comments from American political leaders inflamed American domestic opinion towards the Commonwealth. Therefore, it is logical to conclude that Attlee's perception of American comments reduced the coalition's unity. Furthermore, Taft's comment likely created Commonwealth confusion regarding Truman's statements that outlined his intent to limit the war to Korea and concern regarding American will to secure its allies in Europe. However, American political leaders needed something to support their claims. MacArthur provided sufficient evidence.

---

[269]U.S. Department of State, *Foreign Relations of the United States 1950,* vol. 3, 1700.

MacArthur's comments before and after his dismissal inspired the negative remarks from American political leaders. Therefore, it is reasonable to conclude that MacArthur's public statements did more to inflame American domestic opinion to the Commonwealth and harm coalition unity than comments by American politicians and former presidents. Combined, these separate statements reduced American popular support for the war and, according to Attlee's perception, damaged coalition unity. MacArthur, as the military commander, retains the majority of blame for this.

The seven months between Chinese intervention and MacArthur's dismissal exemplify the military commander's critical role in a coalition operation. The commander's responsibility is to accomplish the coalition mission. However, commanders also have a responsibility to sustain coalition unity. It is logical to believe that the military commander plays a more important role in sustaining coalition than the political leader. Therefore, a coalition's unity of effort heavily depends on more than the military commander's operational or strategic acumen. It also relies on that commander's political awareness and, thus, the commander's willingness and ability to sustain the coalition through their public statements.

MacArthur's claim that Europe's demise was "inevitable"[270] if Asia fell to communism appears to present an understanding of coalition member concerns. The Attlee government, for example, was worried about Western Europe's security. It shared Truman's goal of localizing the war in Korea to defend better Western Europe. However, MacArthur's statement indicated his lack of consideration for his partners' apprehensions

_____

[270]U.S. Department of State, Foreign Policy Studies Branch, Chronology of Principle Events Relating to the Korean Conflict, March 1951, 33.

and, thus, increased Commonwealth "misgivings"[271] about his true intentions in Korea. His subsequent statements did not soothe these Commonwealth fears.

For example, MacArthur, as the coalition's military commander, publicly identified Acheson's goal to "hold a line" and force the Chinese to negotiate as an unacceptable stalemate. Conversely, Matthew Ridgway, commanding all ground forces, felt this course of action represented a "tremendous victory."[272] MacArthur's comment revealed an inclination to make decisions on his own without consideration for the coalition's political goals or unity. It increased his untrustworthiness within the coalition. A coalition commander considered untrustworthy by a coalition will hurt the coalition's unity of effort and prompt contributing nations to reconsider their assistance. Unfortunately, a Truman comment in November 1950 nearly created similar consequences.

Truman remarked that he was considering all possible means to stop the Chinese, "including the atomic bomb,"[273] during a November 30, 1950 press conference. Truman's statement brought his Commonwealth partners' "anxiety to a climax."[274] His advisors quickly sought to reverse the damage caused by his statement. They announced that the use of an atomic bomb was a presidential decision, and that Truman did not

---

[271]Stairs, *The Diplomacy of Constraint: Canada, the Korean War, and the United States*, 132.

[272]U.S. Department of State, Foreign Policy Studies Branch, Chronology of Principle Events Relating to the Korean Conflict, March 1951, iv.

[273]Ferrell, *Off the Record. The Private Papers of Harry S. Truman*, 202.

[274]Fitzsimmons, *The Foreign Policy of the British Labour Government 1945-1951*, 138.

delegate responsibility for this decision to MacArthur for operations in Korea.[275]

Truman's advisors made these statements to soothe Commonwealth fears that "MacArthur was running the show"[276] in Korea without presidential restrictions. Unfortunately, Truman's comment created a Commonwealth perception that he wanted to use atomic weapons in Korea regardless of that decision's potential negative consequences, such as Soviet interference in Korea.

The Commonwealth nations, already fearful of a wider war, felt that using atomic bombs in Korea would induce a Soviet atomic retaliation against Western Europe.[277] Truman's statement, thus, appeared to confirm Commonwealth concerns that the war would escalate into a wider conflict.[278] Attlee demonstrated the Commonwealth's anxiety by rushing almost immediately to the United States in December 1950 to conduct "intimate discussions" with the American President and ensure that the coalition did not reach a "point of no return" in Korea.[279] Furthermore, Attlee revealed Commonwealth anxiety by informing Truman that over one hundred members of the British Parliament protested his statement that suggested the use of atomic bombs in Korea.[280]

---

[275]Truman, *Memoirs by Harry S. Truman, Volume II: Years of Trial and Hope,* 396.

[276]Lowe, "The Korean war in Anglo-US Relations, 1950-53," 130.

[277]Dockrill, *British Defence since 1945,* 43.

[278]O'Neill, *Australia in the Korean War 1950-53. Volume I: Strategy and Diplomacy,* 145.

[279]U.S. Department of State, *Foreign Relations of the United States 1950,* vol. 3, 1698-99.

[280]U.S. Department of State, Foreign Policy Studies Branch, Chronology of Principle Events Relating to the Korean Conflict, December 1950, 5.

St Laurent's government also protested Truman's statement. St Laurent argued that the use of atomic bombs, regardless of the location, was a matter of world concern. Therefore, according to St Laurent's government, Truman could not reserve for the United States the authority to use atomic bombs in Korea.[281] Truman's "categorical statement"[282] appeared to ignore his partners' perspectives and aggravated the coalition's decreasing unity of effort.

Coalition partners need to understand the coalition's objective. Furthermore, they need to achieve common understanding concerning the ways and means to achieve those objectives. This understanding was evident when the UN resolved to repel North Korea's invasion of the ROK. However, the coalition did not establish a common understanding of the ways and means to achieve the subsequent UN mandate to unify all of Korea. Truman's comment gave the impression that he felt his nation's "lead nation" status for UN operations in Korea allowed his administration to make decisions without consulting its coalition partners. Truman's statement did not cause the UN coalition to dissolve. However, it created additional tension between the United States and its Commonwealth partners.

Partners such as Attlee continued efforts to show their nation's solidarity with the United States "in fair or foul weather."[283] As previously stated, Britain recognized the

---

[281]U.S. Department of State, Foreign Policy Studies Branch, Chronology of Principle Events Relating to the Korean Conflict, December 1950, 13.

[282]Memo for the Files, Papers of George M. Elsey, Harry S. Truman Library, Independence, MO.

[283]U.S. Department of State, Foreign Policy Studies Branch, Chronology of Principle Events Relating to the Korean Conflict, December 1950, 15.

Communist Chinese government to protect its economic interests on mainland China. However, Attlee's government employed economic means to limit China's military capabilities when its intervention became likely. First, it stopped shipping oil to China.[284] Later, Attlee's government only shipped oil to China that was "clearly marked for civilian use" in an effort to prevent its use by the Chinese military while sustaining Britain's commercial interests in China.[285]

Attlee clearly wanted to prove Britain's friendship with the United States. His sanctions against China hurt an American enemy but presented a significant risk to Britain's economic stability. Therefore, one can reasonably conceive that Attlee did everything in his power to prove his nation's camaraderie with the United States. However, factors outside of the war in Korea motivated Attlee to ensure that Truman's administration recognized British dependability.

Attlee needed American support to protect Britain and Western Europe from Soviet aggression. Acheson informed Attlee that this would be impossible "unless America's allies gave full support to American policy in East Asia."[286] This statement reflected the Truman administration's perception, identified when it was developing a coalition, that it could use its preponderance of forces and materiél to subjugate its coalition partners to American will. Therefore, Attlee found himself in a situation where,

---

[284]Memorandum of Conversation: Oil to China, with Sir Oliver Franks, July 16, 1950, Papers of Dean Acheson, Harry S. Truman Library, Independence, MO.

[285]U.S. Department of State, World Reaction to President's Statement, No. 12, July 9, 1950.

[286]Lowe, "The Significance of the Korean War in Anglo-American Relations, 1950-53," 129.

107

in seeking an ally's critical support for his national defense, he felt compelled to reduce his own nation's capacity for self-defense to support that same ally in a theater of war that did not directly threaten British security.

MacArthur's character and statements eventually appeared to represent the worst component of that partnership to the Commonwealth governments. The Commonwealth nations felt MacArthur's "unrivalled experience"[287] made him in June 1950 the best choice for Supreme Commander of UN forces in Korea. However, admiration developed into hesitancy. Commonwealth leaders likely did not contribute forces to Korea to expose their personnel to MacArthur's conceited personality. Furthermore, Commonwealth leaders likely did not contribute forces to Korea to achieve an objective that they did not support.

MacArthur, as discussed, noticeably increased Commonwealth apprehensions of his personal goals. Specifically, MacArthur's comments indicated that he wanted to expand the war in Korea to "dispose of the 'Chinese Communist question' once and for all."[288] Therefore, the Commonwealth governments eventually came to realize that their military forces were fighting under a commander who did not share the coalition's goals to localize the war to Korea and preserve South Korea's government. Truman dismissed MacArthur in April 1951 to ensure that Commonwealth leaders did not have "doubt or confusion as to the real purpose and aim of our policy."[289]

---

[287]Ibid., 128.

[288]Melady, *Korea: Canada's Forgotten War*, 87.

[289]U.S. Department of State, Foreign Policy Studies Branch, Chronology of Principle Events Relating to the Korean Conflict, April 1951, 15.

The Commonwealth governments "favorably received" news of MacArthur's dismissal.[290] The St Laurent government's reaction, for example, was one of simple relief that MacArthur was now incapable of escalating the war in Korea.[291] Menzies demonstrated "evident relief"[292] that Ridgway, a commander more disposed to enhancing coalition unity, was now in command. Menzies continued to promise Australia's full support and cooperation for whomever Truman selected to command the UN coalition.

These examples highlight the military commander's important responsibilities within a coalition. A coalition commander cannot, as MacArthur did, develop a "fuehrer complex"[293] and think their understanding of the military situation warrants their dictating policy or defining objectives. The military commander is a critical asset for maintaining a coalition's unity of effort. This asset becomes even more significant if a coalition's objective changes, as it did in Korea. The commander cannot, as MacArthur did, become "isolated from representatives"[294] of contributing nations. Specific to changes in strategic goals, coalition commanders must engage and reengage their multinational partners to sustain unity and, thus, prompt contributing nations to continue providing assets to accomplish the mission. MacArthur's actions in Korea, therefore, reflect what should not occur within a coalition framework.

---

[290]Ibid., 24.

[291]Melady, *Korea: Canada's Forgotten War*, 88.

[292]O'Neill, *Australia in the Korean War 1950-53. Volume I: Strategy and Diplomacy*, 208.

[293]U.S. Department of State, Foreign Policy Studies Branch, Chronology of Principle Events Relating to the Korean Conflict, April 1951, 44.

[294]Grey, *The Commonwealth Armies and the Korean War*, 116.

109

Amongst the Commonwealth nations, American relations with Canada suffered the most from the Korean War. Attlee understood his nation's reliance on American assistance in Europe. He never lost sight of that reality. Menzies' government conducted its relationship with the Truman administration with the primary goal of signing a Pacific security agreement with the United States. However, according to Lester Pearson, Canada's "relatively easy and automatic political relations"[295] with the United States were finished. Outside of MacArthur's comments, American disparagement of Canadian force contributions created the St Laurent government's critical point of contention with the United States. Specifically, St Laurent's government disliked American references to Canada as a "reluctant friend."[296]

Diplomacy by Truman's administration from the Inchon landings until MacArthur's relief increased Commonwealth apprehensions and, therefore, fractured coalition unity. The haughty attitude of Truman's administration after the Inchon landings guided its efforts to procure further military contributions from the Commonwealth nations. Truman's administration tended to base its opinions of, and conduct towards, its partners on the respective size and timing of each nation's contributions.

The coalition commander could have reduced the effects of the Truman administration's conduct. MacArthur could have used his prestige and influence to engender American public and political appreciation for Commonwealth contributions.

---

[295] John W. Holmes, "Canada and the United States in World Politics," *Foreign Affairs* 40, no. 1 (October 1961): 105.

[296] U.S. Department of State, Foreign Policy Studies Branch, Chronology of Principle Events Relating to the Korean Conflict, April 1951, 19.

However, he did not. Coalition unity, as a result, continued to dissolve under his leadership. The Truman administration's decisiveness after North Korea's invasion of South Korea demonstrated an American intent to contain communism. Unfortunately, the Truman administration's self-important conduct forced its Commonwealth partners to obsess over not if, but how, the United States would respond to international security concerns and the roles it would expect its Commonwealth partners to perform.[297]

---

[297]Melady, *Korea: Canada's Forgotten War*, 88.

CHAPTER 4

COALITION SUSTAINMENT AND THE MILITARY

Coalition Integration, Combat, and Koje-Do

The Americans were paying most of the piper's bill. It followed that they were calling most of the piper's tunes.
— Denis Stairs, "Canada and the Korean War Fifty Years On"

Jeffrey Grey stated that military alliances or coalitions are likely to lose unity if the organization's internal balance of power "shifts decisively" towards one member nation.[298] Evidence suggests that the United States-led coalition in Korea validates Grey's argument. At the political level, previous chapters demonstrated that President Harry Truman's administration did not always understand its coalition partners' limitations and, thus, failed to treat them with patience or respect. From a military perspective, American leaders appeared to use their nation's dominance in personnel and materiél to dictate operations and expect coalition compliance for these tasks without regard for coalition partner perspectives. American behavior and the Commonwealth's perceptions of American battlefield incompetence, therefore, increased the tensions developed through diplomatic activities.

A "military superiority complex"[299] explained the conduct of American military leaders and soldiers towards their Commonwealth partners in Korea. This mindset of superiority is understandable under two conditions. First, it is reasonable if one is

---

[298]Grey, *The Commonwealth Armies and the Korean War* (Manchester, UK: Manchester University Press, 1988), 6.

[299]Blair, *The Forgotten War: America in Korea 1950-1953*, 78.

112

discussing military operations prior to the Chinese invasion of Korea in November 1950. A coalition predominantly comprised of American forces rapidly landed at Inchon, captured Seoul, crossed the 38th Parallel, and appeared unstoppable in its effort to unify the Korean peninsula. Second, this perspective is fathomable if one considers that the United States provided over seventy percent of the UN coalition's combat forces by July 1951. Conversely, all foreign nations, excluding the Republic of Korea, provided just over six percent of the UN combat forces.[300]

The general viewpoints of the United States military commanders in Korea were negligible by July 1951. China's military successes should have sufficed to remove perceptions of American invincibility. During the Chinese invasion, Commonwealth forces observed American military units retreating "in jeeps and trucks from an overwhelming horde of poorly equipped Chinese . . . following on mules, ponies and camels."[301] Therefore, the Chinese invasion destroyed notions of America's military invincibility to its Commonwealth partners. However, Commonwealth perceptions of American incompetence did not stop American military leaders from showing a "penchant for senior commanders to play squad leader."[302] This tendency alienated their Commonwealth partners.

---

[300]Grey, *The Commonwealth Armies and the Korean War*, 30.

[301]Gallaway, *The Last Call of the Bugle: The Long Road to Kapyong*, 170.

[302]Blaxland, "The Korean War: Reflections on Shared Australian and Canadian Military Experiences," 31.

Coalition members expect the lead nation to possess sufficient "will and capability, competence, and influence"[303] to lead coalition operations. Traits such as these engender support for the lead nation from its coalition partners. Coalition unity and resolve, thus, depend partially on the lead nation's military competence. Therefore, military incompetence or failures from the lead nation are likely to affect negatively coalition unity and the lead nation's ability to lead the coalition.

The military forces a state contributes to a coalition represent its government and population. This fact is even more critical regarding the lead nation's forces. The lead nation government expects its military's actions to represent its resolve and competence to lead the coalition to accomplish its mission. Military competence from the lead nation's forces indirectly reflects the significance that nation places upon the coalition's mission to its coalition partners. Furthermore, lead nation military competence indirectly demonstrates to coalition partners that the lead nation is politically and militarily capable of leading the coalition to accomplish its mission. Conversely, military incompetence from the lead nation's military forces encourages the likely development of three negative perceptions within the coalition's other members.

First, military incompetence is likely to raise coalition concerns about the lead nation's willingness to accomplish the coalition's mission. Lead nations that contribute other than their best forces appear less than fully committed to mission accomplishment. Second, operational or tactical failures are likely to force contributing nations' governments to reconsider their perspective of the mission. Therefore, these nations may

---

[303] Chairman, Joint Chiefs of Staff, Joint Publication 3-16, *Multinational Operations* (Washington, DC: Government Printing Office, 2013), C-3.

be motivated to withdraw their force contributions due to perceptions of lead nation

military incompetence. Third, lead nation military failures or incompetence are likely to

heighten anxiety in the soldiers committed by contributing nations. These soldiers are

likely to question the lead nation's military leadership, decision-making and, therefore,

their role within the coalition if the lead nation's military leadership exhibits

incompetence. All of these conditions negatively affect a coalition's unity of effort.

Operations in Korea demonstrated these conditions.

Militarily, three additional areas of concern contributed to a declining unity of

effort within the UN coalition in Korea. United States policy for Korea created the first

concern. American integration of Commonwealth forces upon their arrival to Korea,

specifically Canada's, created the second concern. Finally, different approaches to tactics

created the third concern.

The Truman administration reversed its policy of "rollback," whereby it sought to

unify the Korean peninsula under one noncommunist government, to a defense of the

"status quo antebellum" in November 1951.[304] The administration's new goal sought to

inflict maximum Chinese losses in personnel and materiél "to create conditions

favourable [*sic*] to a settlement of the Korean conflict."[305] Therefore, Truman's

administration reverted to the original UN mandate of retaining South Korea's

sovereignty. The third chapter of this thesis provided details and analysis on the

administration's decision to cross the 38th Parallel and the effects of that decision on

---

[304]Grey, *The Commonwealth Armies and the Korean War*, 46.

[305]Johnston, *A War of Patrols: Canadian Army Operations in Korea*, 127.

coalition unity. The Truman administration's reversal, consequently, created a similar effect on coalition unity.

Truman's administration decided to seek a settlement in Korea in November 1951. Its decision constituted the administration's second major policy change for operations on the peninsula. However, it decided on this verdict after "many American units had performed badly"[306] while retreating from the Chinese advance. This is problematic for two reasons.

First, Truman's administration allowed military events to dictate its decision-making methodology and policies. For example, successful post-Inchon operations encouraged Truman's administration to seek Korean unification. Additionally, failures following the Chinese landings motivated the Truman administration's decision to seek a negotiated settlement. Therefore, Truman's administration created Commonwealth perceptions of American uncertainty and hesitancy rather than American resolve and decisiveness. The coalition objective for Korea, a political goal, should never have changed. At minimum, military circumstances should not dictate the political objective. Maintaining one objective typically leads to a quicker conclusion of events and, thus, encourages retention of coalition unity.

Second, the Truman administration's decision to maintain the status quo in Korea negatively affected the morale of Commonwealth soldiers. Australian soldiers, for example, volunteered to serve in Korea "to fight."[307] They did not volunteer to maintain a

---

[306]Grey, *The Commonwealth Armies and the Korean War*, 85.

[307]Gallaway, *The Last Call of the Bugle: The Long Road to Kapyong*, 52.

status quo that "appeared to be a waste of lives"[308] while diplomats pursued a negotiated settlement. General Matthew Ridgway, upon assuming command of the EUSA in December 1950, felt that American soldiers were unprepared "mentally and spiritually"[309] to seek a decisive victory in Korea. Politically, Truman's decision to seek a negotiated settlement demonstrated his mental and spiritual unwillingness in 1951 to unify Korea.

Soldiers, regardless of the era, are uninterested in conducting military operations to allow political leaders to "save face."[310] Conscripted soldiers must fight regardless of the circumstances. However, volunteers typically offer to fight because they believe in the war's purpose. They will not provide their unquestioned allegiance to the lead nation's military commander or to the coalition's mission if they perceive the war as futile. Regardless, Commonwealth soldiers found their unity with the United States government and the UN Command tested almost immediately after arriving in Korea.

Commonwealth soldiers characterized their initial employment in Korea as a great deal of "ad hocery [*sic*]."[311] The combat situation the Commonwealth soldiers faced upon their arrival to the Korean peninsula likely created this depiction. British forces, for example, arrived before the Inchon landings. The coalition's situation remained perilous at this time. The attitude of American military leaders was that "a little got in fast was

---

[308]Trembath, *A Different Sort of War: Australians in Korea 1950-53*, 143.

[309]Ridgway, *The Korean War*, 86.

[310]Trembath, *A Different Sort of War: Australians in Korea 1950-53*, 143.

[311]Grey, *The Commonwealth Armies and the Korean War*, 46.

better than a lot later on."[312] Therefore, coalition commanders frequently rushed Commonwealth soldiers into combat without sufficient preparation. Specifically, leaders such as General Douglas MacArthur wanted all Commonwealth troops sent to Korea to engage immediately in combat without conducting pre-combat training or terrain familiarization.

It is standard for incoming units and personnel to conduct training before entering combat. United States Army units deployed to Iraq or Afghanistan, for example, did not immediately undertake combat missions upon arriving to their respective theater. They verified the accuracy of their weapons, received intelligence and threat briefings, and conducted other training as required before taking on their mission. This method of introducing soldiers to combat is typical throughout American history.

However, the American-led coalition in Korea faced dire military situations prior to the Inchon landings and after the Chinese invasion. MacArthur's policy of assigning troops to combat positions immediately after arriving to Korea presented clear risk to those soldiers' lives and to the good of the mission. However, MacArthur's strategy in this example is understandable. Military necessity required as many troops as possible from the UN Command engaging the DPRK's army in combat. Furthermore, Commonwealth governments should have ensured that their forces were prepared sufficiently before deploying to Korea to allay concerns regarding MacArthur's approach. Canadian forces deploying to Korea illustrated this responsibility.

---

[312]Farrar-Hockley, *The British Part in the Korean War, Volume I: A Distant Obligation*, 119.

The 2 PPCLI departed for Korea on November 25.[313] 2 PPCLI expected to complete collective training in Korea and subsequently to perform occupation duties. The UN Command's favorable military circumstances from the Inchon landings until late November 1950 justified the battalion's expectations. However, the Chinese invaded Korea on the same day 2 PPCLI departed for Korea.[314] China's invasion delayed hopes for a quick UN victory. Therefore, 2 PPCLI, having conducted minimal collective training prior to its departure for Korea, faced unexpected tasks for which it was unprepared upon arriving to the peninsula.[315]

The 2 PPCLI's unanticipated situation did not deter the EUSA Commander, Lieutenant General Walton Walker, from seeking its immediate employment in battle. Walker wanted 2 PPCLI to occupy a "reserve position not far from the battleline [*sic*]"[316] upon its arrival. Walker died before writing a memoir. His personal thoughts regarding the employment of Canadian or other Commonwealth forces, therefore, are unrecorded.

It is likely that Walker felt his placement of 2 PPCLI in a reserve location, rather than a front-line position, was sufficient compromise for 2 PPCLI's unpreparedness. Regardless, 2 PPCLI's leadership perceived that Walker wanted the battalion engaged without sufficient preparation. Walker's alleged spirit of "defeatism"[317] in the aftermath

---

[313]Stairs, *The Diplomacy of Constraint: Canada, the Korean War, and the United States*, 206.

[314]Johnston, *A War of Patrols: Canadian Army Operations in Korea*, 55.

[315]Watson, *Far Eastern Tour: The Canadian Infantry in Korea, 1950-1953*, 177.

[316]Stairs, *The Diplomacy of Constraint: Canada, the Korean War, and the United States*, 206.

[317]Johnston, *A War of Patrols: Canadian Army Operations in Korea*, 55.

of China's invasion likely clouded his judgment regarding the employment of incoming Commonwealth forces. The Canadians appeared to reach this conclusion.

Lieutenant-Colonel J.R. Stone served as the 2 PPCLI commander when the battalion arrived to Korea. Stone's orders from the Canadian government directed him to conduct an eight-week training period after arriving to Korea. Additionally, Louis St Laurent's government ordered Stone to avoid combat operations except for cases of self-defense and until he felt satisfied that 2 PPCLI was "fit for operations."[318] These orders, therefore, created a conflict of interest between Stone and American commanders such as Walker. This conflict was avoidable.

As stated, 2 PPCLI believed that it would conduct occupation duties after arriving to Korea. This understanding came from the combat situation that existed when 2 PPCLI departed North America and from the St Laurent government's expectations. Stone cannot receive fault for being unfamiliar with the combat situation upon his arrival to Korea. The Chinese did not invade until his unit was seaborne. Stone, thus, logically believed that current operations would reach a successful conclusion while his unit was in transit to Korea.

Conversely, Truman's administration and St Laurent's government failed to achieve a shared understanding of expectations. Dean Acheson continually emphasized the "importance that everyone contribute as much as they could,"[319] during his

---

[318]Stairs, *The Diplomacy of Constraint: Canada, the Korean War, and the United States*, 206.

[319]Memorandum of Conversation: Formosa, Contribution of Troops by Canada, between Dean Acheson and Lester B. Pearson, July 29, 1950, Papers of Dean Acheson, Harry S. Truman Library, Independence, MO.

conversations with Lester Pearson, Canada's Minister for External Affairs, from June until November 1950. Therefore, it is logical to conclude that Truman's administration felt it reached a common understanding of expectations with St Laurent's government after that government announced its intention to provide land forces to Korea. Canadian troops were clearly unprepared for combat. Regardless, political necessities forced St Laurent's government to rush Canadian land forces to Korea.

The St Laurent government's expectations of an eight-week training period for 2 PPCLI after its arrival to Korea demonstrates the haste with which it decided to contribute land forces to Korea. Canadian expectations also portray a government that did not share common understanding with Truman's administration. St Laurent's government should have expected that its land forces would face some form of combat regardless of the positive situation that existed when they departed for Korea. Unfortunately, this lack of understanding adversely contributed to poor relations between American and Canadian military leaders.

Stone had to negotiate with Walker to ensure 2 PPCLI conducted its government-mandated training period upon arrival. At times, Stone felt forced to present Walker with his government's specific orders "to substantiate his negotiating position"[320] and thereby meet his government's expectations. The fact that Stone felt required to resort to such measures, despite the perilous combat situation, demonstrates a lack of American patience and poor knowledge of partners at the military level. Additionally, Walker's

---

[320]Stairs, *The Diplomacy of Constraint: Canada, the Korean War, and the United States*, 206.

impatience and minimal knowledge regarding a coalition partner reflected a lack of respect for that partner's national concerns and limitations.

Walker's command finally agreed to Stone's training timeline for two reasons. The first was political: Walker could not completely disregard the orders of a coalition partner's government. Second, Walker recognized that, by giving Stone what he wanted, a training period would "hasten" 2 PPCLI's "arrival to the front."[321] Walker demonstrated less than mere patience or respect for a coalition partner's contributions. His command ignored the "moral flavor"[322] that multinational contributions, regardless of type or size, provided to a UN coalition operating under United States leadership. Furthermore, Walker's impatience and lack of respect appeared to permeate through most American units and their tactical expectations for Commonwealth forces.

Jeffrey Grey argued that the EUSA placed Commonwealth forces in situations "above and beyond that which they should've been called to face."[323] Specifically, American commanders typically employed Commonwealth forces as a "rearguard" force for American units.[324] According to Grey, these situations were "above and beyond" because the Commonwealth forces were "smaller"[325] than American units and, thus, lacked sufficient personnel and matériel to conform to United States Army doctrine. Therefore, according to Grey, EUSA expected too much from the Commonwealth forces'

---

[321]Johnston, *A War of Patrols: Canadian Army Operations in Korea*, 55.

[322]Ridgway, *The Korean War*, 148.

[323]Grey, *The Commonwealth Armies and the Korean War*, 8.

[324]Grey, *A Military History of Australia*, 205.

[325]Blaxland, "The Korean War: Reflections on Shared Australian and Canadian Military Experiences," 30.

minimal capabilities. Regardless, Commonwealth units believed that their American partners lacked combat skills and willpower to fight.

Some Commonwealth soldiers, such as Anthony Farrar-Hockley, felt this American problem resided at the highest echelons of command. Specifically, Farrar-Hockley argued that MacArthur's desire to replicate the "brilliance"[326] he demonstrated during and immediately after the Inchon landing created poor methods of American strategic and tactical planning. Other Commonwealth personnel felt the issue lay at the military's lower levels, specifically after the Chinese invasion and the "poor American combat performance"[327] during that period.

Bluntly, the British and Australian militaries' confidence in United States land forces "declined considerably"[328] after the Chinese invasion. Canadian land forces had yet to engage in combat during this time. However, British and Australian soldiers identified "widespread panic"[329] in their American counterparts and felt that American reports on the Chinese advance were "fabrications . . . to gain permission for premature and quite unjustifiable withdrawals."[330] Ridgway, replacing Walker as EUSA commander, appeared to support these conclusions in *The Korean War*. Ridgway

---

[326]Farrar-Hockley, *The British Part in the Korean War, Volume I: A Distant Obligation*, 206.

[327]Grey, *The Commonwealth Armies and the Korean War*, 87.

[328]Jeffrey Grey, "The Regiment's First War: Korea, 1950-56," in *Duty First. A History of the Royal Australian Regiment*, eds. David Horner and Jean Bou (New South Wales: Allen & Unwin, 2008), 66.

[329]Johnston, *A War of Patrols: Canadian Army Operations in Korea*, 56.

[330]Ibid.

believed that his soldiers' "infantry ancestors would roll over in their graves" if they could see their offspring's poor terrain utilization, reluctance to "put shoe leather to earth," and failure, or perhaps unwillingness, to gain and maintain contact with enemy forces.[331] Commonwealth opinions of American military ineptitude, therefore, were not baseless.

Guidance provided by American military commanders further eroded Commonwealth trust and confidence in American military competence. Two examples explain the Commonwealth's reduced trust and confidence. Patrol guidance, issued in May 1952, is the first example. The second example is the decision to remove forces after the battle near Kap'yong. These examples, from a Commonwealth perspective, demonstrated an American inclination to command through "impulsive judgments"[332] and an American reluctance to "stand and fight."[333]

Patrol guidance issued in May 1952 dictated that battalions on the front line conduct at least "one strong fighting patrol per week against recognized enemy positions" and capture at least one prisoner every three days.[334] This policy was unpopular within the Commonwealth formations for various reasons. A primary reason for this policy's unpopularity within the Commonwealth forces was its origination from American staff officers who preferred to remain in their headquarters rather than visit subordinate

---

[331]Ridgway, *The Korean War*, 88-89.

[332]Farrar-Hockley, *The British Part in the Korean War, Volume I: A Distant Obligation*, 336.

[333]Grey, "The Regiment's First War: Korea, 1950-56," 66.

[334]Watson, *Far Eastern Tour: The Canadian Infantry in Korea, 1950-1953*, 80.

formations.[335] These staff officers, according to Commonwealth soldiers, were unfamiliar with realities faced by lower echelons of command. Therefore, Commonwealth commanders argued for guidance to conduct patrols "according to the tactical situation at hand, rather than adhering to a rigid timetable."[336] Their frustration with this decision-making methodology increased after Kap'yong.

The Commonwealth's critical contention regarding Kap'yong originated with the American willingness to abandon the UN position in that area after fighting concluded. The Commonwealth's military commanders considered the withdrawal unnecessary, specifically because it surrendered "hard-won territory without a fight."[337] Furthermore, the battle and subsequent withdrawal of UN forces reflected differences between American and Commonwealth approaches to combat and EUSA's "continuing reliance" on Commonwealth brigades.[338]

It is common for military formations to complain about their higher headquarters' lack of understanding for their respective situation. Complaints of this nature reflect one of two realities. First, the lower command fails to understand the higher command's objectives and perspectives. The higher command, for example, worries about more than one subordinate formation. Conversely, Ridgway himself lamented several staffs'

[335]Grey, *The Commonwealth Armies and the Korean War*, 70.

[336]Watson, *Far Eastern Tour: The Canadian Infantry in Korea, 1950-1953*, 80.

[337]Johnston, *A War of Patrols: Canadian Army Operations in Korea*, 107.

[338]Grey, *The Commonwealth Armies and the Korean War*, 81.

"unwillingness . . . to forgo certain creature comforts" after he arrived to Korea.[339]

Therefore, Commonwealth complaints of American staff officers were not baseless.

American patrolling guidance showed a lack of knowledge, patience and respect for coalition partners. Furthermore, the decision to withdraw forces from Kap'yong reflects a poor decision-making methodology. Importantly, these examples reflect a United States military command that was not coordinated or unified with its coalition partners. Canadians, for example, did not patrol with vigor.[340] Conversely, Australian forces "patrolled too aggressively."[341] Patrol guidance, thus, did not consider each nation's capabilities, intentions, or limitations.

Australian forces patrolled aggressively because their commanders felt that method provided the "only means to detect China's hidden forces"[342] and engage them in combat. Australian commanders, therefore, could interpret American guidance in one of two ways. First, they could consider the guidance as an American effort to contain Australian forces from opportunities to achieve battlefield "glory" for Australia. Conversely, the American command possibly applied specific patrolling guidance with Australian forces in mind. The Australian proclivity to become "dangerously overextended"[343] explains this possibility.

---

[339]Ridgway, *The Korean War*, 88.

[340]Grey, *The Commonwealth Armies and the Korean War*, 151.

[341]Ibid., 153.

[342]Gallaway, *The Last Call of the Bugle: The Long Road to Kapyong*, 145.

[343]Watson, *Far Eastern Tour: The Canadian Infantry in Korea, 1950-1953*, 93.

Nevertheless, the American military represented the coalition's lead nation and, thus, made the decisions on operations. American military commanders also controlled access to the press and, thus, controlled press releases to nations throughout the world regarding the situation in Korea. The possible Australian interpretation that American commanders felt the United States should receive all credit for positive battlefield activities is understandable. The interpretation is logical when one considers Australia's 1st and 3rd Battalions, Royal Australian Regiment's (1/3 RAR) competent performances as one of EUSA's "more reliable rearguards."[344] Therefore, an Australian interpretation of doing the "dirty work" for the American military is plausible.

The RAR's leaders and soldiers could also interpret American patrolling guidance as an implication that senior American commanders felt Australians were not sufficiently aggressive and, therefore, not supporting their "numerical weight"[345] of the coalition's combat burden. Given the American military's poor performance during its retreat from the Chinese invasion, the majority of 1 and 3 RAR soldiers felt their forces were superior to American military units "in matters of field craft, tactics, or organization [*sic*]."[346] 3 RAR could define either interpretation as an insult from its American commanders. 2 PPCLI, on the other hand, viewed American patrolling guidance from a different perspective.

---

[344]Johnston, *A War of Patrols: Canadian Army Operations in Korea*, 56.

[345]Trembath, *A Different Sort of War: Australians in Korea 1950-53*, 137.

[346]Ibid.

American commanders viewed 2 PPCLI's leadership as excessively concerned with a "spit and polish"[347] garrison mentality and less concerned with fighting and patrolling. In September 1952, for example, 2 PPCLI conducted two fighting patrols and ten ambush patrols. Conversely, 1 RAR conducted twenty-seven fighting patrols and twenty-eight ambush patrols within the first three weeks of September 1952.[348] Therefore, this data makes understandable an American military perception of Canadian military inactivity. The data also presents as logical the American establishment of patrolling guidance specifically directed towards Canadian forces. However, this sentiment neglects an important aspect of Canadian policy.

St Laurent's government sent Canadian forces to Korea to operate under the "control and authority of the United Nations."[349] Canadian forces, thus, did not go to Korea to serve as an American puppet. Therefore, St Laurent's government sought "to preserve a distinctly Canadian position"[350] by maintaining its military's independence in Korea. Therefore, 2 PPCLI and other Canadian forces barely coordinated their actions and operations with their adjacent Commonwealth units. Those forces were "less than amused" by their perceptions of Canadian military ineptitude.[351]

2 PPCLI and subsequent Canadian forces likely did not want, and appeared to accept barely, patrolling guidance from American commanders. Two reasons explain this

---

[347]Johnston, *A War of Patrols: Canadian Army Operations in Korea*, 255.

[348]Ibid., 303.

[349]Melady, *Korea: Canada's Forgotten War*, 72.

[350]Grey, *The Commonwealth Armies and the Korean War*, 131.

[351]Johnston, *A War of Patrols: Canadian Army Operations in Korea*, 316.

perception. First, Canadian military leaders knew the Chinese were "specially trained and equipped . . . while they themselves performed what amounted to a routine task with routine equipment."[352] Canadian forces, thus, did not find logic in operations that offered minimal gains for an objective that sought the status quo antebellum. Second, Canadian leaders understood that American patrolling guidance reduced their forces' independence. Reduced Canadian independence negated St Laurent's perceived "entitlement to join in the policy-making game"[353] after the conflict in Korea concluded.

St Laurent's example of a national government seeking to maintain an independent military within a coalition is not new. President Woodrow Wilson pursued this status after providing American forces to the Anglo-French coalition during the First World War. Specifically, Wilson wanted his armed forces to be "an instrument of the policy of the United States,"[354] independent of British or French command. He expected this independence to combine with a quality battlefield performance that would create for him a strong role "in the peace negotiations that followed the war."[355] St Laurent's government simply followed a pattern established by its American cousins 35 years prior to Korea.

However, American commanders in Korea reacted to Canadian desires in a manner similar to British and French military leaders in World War I. American military

---

[352]Watson, *Far Eastern Tour: The Canadian Infantry in Korea, 1950-1953*, 95.

[353]Denis Stairs, "Canada and the Korean War Fifty Years On," *Canadian Military History* 9, no. 3 (Summer, 2000): 50.

[354]Mitchell A. Yockelson, *Borrowed Soldiers: Americans under British Command, 1918* (Norman: University of Oklahoma Press), 10.

[355]Ibid., xi.

leaders continued to insist on Canadian adherence to American policy and frequently complained of receiving "insufficient information" from Canadian patrols.[356] Unfortunately, "attitudes, tactics, and style,"[357] rather than substance, appear to explain American-Canadian military interactions in Korea. Thus, American-Canadian disagreements appeared to be less about actual tactics and employment and more about the struggle between a coalition member seeking to retain its independence from a coalition leader that wanted to dominate its partners.

American commanders, by employing this method of leadership, forgot that war is "a continuation of political activity by other means."[358] Carl von Clausewitz's definition of war applies to one's interactions with coalition partners as much as it does to one's enemy. American commanders appeared to interact with their Commonwealth partners by following a behavioral precedent established by Dean Acheson. The American military's behavior, thus, appears based on the reputation of military excellence earned after Inchon. The only difference between Acheson and American military leaders was that Acheson demonstrated self-righteous behavior prior to Inchon. American commanders failed to realize that their current situation, created after the Chinese invasion, negated Commonwealth perceptions of American military excellence. The American decision to withdraw UN forces from Kap'yong supports this conclusion.

---

[356]Johnston, *A War of Patrols: Canadian Army Operations in Korea*, 238.

[357]Stairs, *The Diplomacy of Constraint: Canada, the Korean War, and the United States*, 287.

[358]Carl von Clausewitz, *On War*, trans. and eds. Michael Howard and Peter Paret (Princeton: Princeton University Press, 1976), 87.

Truman's administration wanted multinational forces to fight in Korea for two reasons. First, it wanted to ensure that as many UN members as possible represented the coalition. Substantial UN representation enhanced the organization's credibility. Second, the United States could not sustain the manpower burden in Korea by itself. Thus, the American decision to surrender unnecessarily the terrain earned by the UN Command confused the Commonwealth's military forces. This surrender occurred following the battle at Kap'yong.

Commonwealth personnel losses constituted the primary reason for this confusion and concern. The Commonwealth's confusion is specifically understandable if one considers that 3 RAR and 2 PPCLI received a United States Presidential Unit Citation for their efforts at Kap'yong.[359] Thus, they received a significant American military award for actions that did not contribute to the UN Command's long-term success. Therefore, it is rather easy to comprehend Commonwealth confusion and concern with American decision-making.

Minimal personnel limited the Commonwealth's ability to provide military forces for combat operations in Korea. Global commitments, such as the British in Malaya, or Australian and Canadian legislative restrictions to national military sizes created the Commonwealth's limitations. Commonwealth military leaders logically felt that battles that created "equal casualties on both sides" provided an advantage to the Chinese.[360] Their conviction is sensible given China's overwhelming numerical superiority.

---

[359]Melady, *Korea: Canada's Forgotten War*, 78.

[360]Herbert Fairlie Wood, *Strange Battleground: Official History of the Canadian Army in Korea* (Ottawa: Queen's Printer, 1966), 232.

Additionally, China was more capable than UN forces of getting land forces to the Korean battlefield. Therefore, Commonwealth commanders sought to minimize casualties wherever possible. Thus, the Commonwealth's military leaders, having lost substantial manpower at Kap'yong, logically identified the UN withdrawal as an act that did not serve a military purpose.[361]

Commonwealth nations could not afford to sustain "continuous heavy casualties" for military and political reasons.[362] Therefore, Commonwealth disagreements with the withdrawal from Kap'yong are reasonable. Aside from the Commonwealth's personnel constraints, heavy casualties negatively affect a nation's morale. This is true for a nation whether it serves in a coalition as the lead nation or as a subordinate partner. Reduced national morale will affect a nation's policy by demanding a reduction of forces, a removal of all forces, or a change in the command structure. Thus, military commanders within a coalition must always remain cognizant of the effects their operations and decisions will have on popular, political, and military opinions within all contributing nations. Coalition commanders cannot remain concerned with only their nation's morale or willpower.

The majority of American military leaders in Korea appear to have not recognized these facts. MacArthur's autobiography did not comment on the domestic morale of Commonwealth nations when discussing his time in command of UN forces in Korea. He appeared to have been unconcerned about the effects of his operations on domestic

---

[361]Blaxland, "The Korean War: Reflections on Shared Australian and Canadian Military Experiences," 30.

[362]Ibid.

Commonwealth morale or politics. Ridgway appeared to be a leader Commonwealth

soldiers respected for the simple fact that he did not typically order advances unless he

was reasonably certain of gaining ground.[363] Thus, evidence suggests that Ridgway

remained cognizant of sustaining his personnel as a means to preserve politically and

militarily his coalition's unity and morale.

However, the commander's command climate must reflect his command style and

considerations. The Chinese invasion in November 1950 created a war that pitted two

armies "of approximately equal strength and determination" against each other.[364] Thus,

conservation of resources, specifically troops, and military and national morale grew

more crucial as the Korean War continued without an identifiable end in sight. Ridgway

understood this reality. Evidence suggests that Commonwealth forces believed a majority

of American commanders did not adhere to Ridgway's methodology.

British commanders in Korea appeared to understand best this reality. The British

held a reputation of being "slow on offense but unshakable on defense."[365] Their

reputation did not stop British commanders from questioning the "why," or the purpose

and necessity, for American-decided operations.[366] These concepts were not new to

British military doctrine. Field Marshal Bernard Law Montgomery, for example,

---

[363]Gallaway, *The Last Call of the Bugle: The Long Road to Kapyong*, 203.

[364]Weigley, *The American Way of War: A History of United States Military Strategy and Policy*, 393.

[365]Blair, *The Forgotten War. America in Korea 1950-1953*, 825.

[366]Grey, *The Commonwealth Armies and the Korean War*, 138.

continuously sought to "nurture the morale"[367] of his forces during the Second World War by remaining cautious and thereby avoid unnecessary casualties. Fortunately, British traits appear to have not bothered American commanders, other than MacArthur,[368] as much as their other Commonwealth partners.

American commanders and soldiers held a high opinion of their British counterparts because they were reliable in combat, could sustain themselves, and used American-provided equipment in a "highly professional" manner.[369] British military leaders, and their Commonwealth partners, held United States Marines in high regard. Unfortunately, they maintained a considerably negative opinion of soldiers in the American army.[370] Two examples created British contempt for American soldiers. American actions in combat represent the first example. Second, American soldiers behaved poorly when captured by enemy forces.

American commanders exhibited a habit of relying on British forces if American units were in a "sticky situation."[371] This practice likely began after British forces, along with Turkish formations, stood their ground against the initial Chinese invasion while EUSA formations retreated en masse.[372] Thus, according to the British, American

---

[367]Stephen Hart, *Montgomery and Colossal Cracks: the 21st Army Group in Northwest Europe, 1944-45* (Westport, CT: Praeger Publishing, 2000), 114.

[368]Pogue, *George C. Marshall: Statesman, 1945-1959*, 460.

[369]Grey, *The Commonwealth Armies and the Korean War*, 85.

[370]Trembath, *A Different Sort of War: Australians in Korea 1950-53*, 136.

[371]Grey, *The Commonwealth Armies and the Korean War*, 85.

[372]Gallaway, *The Last Call of the Bugle: The Long Road to Kapyong*, 282.

perceptions of military superiority appeared rooted less in substance and more in style. The main problem with these actions was that American soldiers represented the coalition's lead nation and, therefore, the coalition's credibility.

Soldiers sent to combat in distant lands want to know their senior commanders, and the soldiers that represent those commanders, are capable of accomplishing their respective missions. The Commonwealth, as stated, provided just greater than six percent of the UN coalition's combat power compared to America's share of seventy percent. Surely, the British understood the overall limitations preventing the Commonwealth from affecting significantly the course of the war. However, lead nation incompetence in combat, real or perceived, will disrupt the morale of the soldiers contributed by other nations. By extension, reduced morale will affect negatively the national policies within those contributing nations.

The behavior of American prisoners of war (POW) did not increase British or Commonwealth opinions of American military competence. Richard Trembath argued that American soldiers suffered a "total collapse of morale" when captured.[373] That statement does not cite Trembath to infer that all American soldiers acted poorly or without courage when captured. However, British and other Commonwealth soldiers shared this perception of American POWs. British POWs actually requested separation from American POWs for their negative effects on British morale.[374]

This chapter does not argue that all American leaders, soldiers, and organizations performed poorly in Korea. However, statements throughout this chapter discussing

---

[373]Trembath, *A Different Sort of War: Australians in Korea 1950-53*, 83.

[374]Ibid., 84.

Commonwealth criticism of American forces represent Commonwealth perceptions. It is traditional for perceptions to be mistaken for reality. As stated, soldiers representing a coalition's lead nation symbolize that nation's and, thus, the coalition's credibility. Commonwealth perceptions of American combat skill demonstrate minimal credibility for the coalition in Korea.

Evidence indicates that the Commonwealth forces perceived American military ineptness in Korea. In the absence of numerous autobiographies or personal interviews, one can only believe that a substantial number of Commonwealth soldiers, with their perceptions of their American partners, felt concern for their counterparts and, thus, their role in Korea. Specifically, one must believe that those soldiers, perceiving American military leadership and capabilities as inept, questioned their governments' decisions to send them to Korea. This curiosity will never fail to damage coalition unity and, thus, negatively affect the coalition's ability to accomplish its assigned mission. Communication is a critical skill to alleviate these concerns.

Events at Koje-Do represent an incident that would have benefitted from greater communication. Koje-Do was a location responsible for maintaining enemy POWs. The camp held over 160,000 Chinese and North Korean prisoners. 60,000 Koje-Do POWs identified themselves as "anti-communist."[375] The communist majority subjected the non-communist minority to numerous beatings and other intimidation tactics.

The United States was the only nation providing security forces at Koje-Do when harsh communist tactics first occurred. General Mark Wayne Clarke, Ridgway's

---

[375]Stairs, *The Diplomacy of Constraint: Canada, the Korean War, and the United States*, 246.

replacement as commander of all UN forces, wanted to integrate Koje-Do's American security forces with multinational forces to alleviate international pressure on the United States for these actions. Clarke selected Canadian forces, among others, to provide security at Koje-Do. However, Clarke did not consult St Laurent's government prior to this selection.[376]

Clarke was not required to consult with respective governments whose soldiers he assigned to Koje-Do. UN members provided military forces to an American-led coalition to accomplish a mission. Clarke was the military commander of all UN forces. Clarke's responsibility, therefore, was to array his forces in a manner that allowed him to accomplish his assigned mission. This fact applies to any military commander in any combat scenario. Furthermore, prisoner security existed as one of Clarke's essential tasks. His responsibility, again, is a typical obligation for any military commander.

St Laurent's government objected to Clarke's "menial and ignominious"[377] employment of its troops. St Laurent's government registered this protest specifically because Clarke, or another American official, did not consult it beforehand. Canada's official historian, Herbert Fairlie Wood, eventually admitted that St Laurent's government "made too much fuss over the affair."[378] Regardless, Truman's administration identified St Laurent's government as excessively willing to oppose

---

[376]Blaxland, "The Korean War: Reflections on Shared Australian and Canadian Military Experiences," 31.

[377]Stairs, *The Diplomacy of Constraint: Canada, the Korean War, and the United States*, 252.

[378]Wood, *Strange Battleground: Official History of the Canadian Army in Korea*, 196.

diplomatically the United States for simple "political propaganda."[379] Therefore, Canadian protests damaged relations with the Truman administration.

According to Wood, "the vital necessity for prior consultation . . . when unusual activity of any sort is being contemplated" establishes the main lesson from Clarke's actions.[380] Wood's argument is not completely erroneous. Had Clarke understood St Laurent's position, specifically regarding the independence of Canadian formations within the UN Command, this problem likely would not have occurred. However, circumstances that represent "unusual activity" always occur in war. Regardless, Wood's standards for "unusual activity" do not apply to prisoner of war security.

Prisoner of war security is a standard military task. All soldiers, and the governments that send them to war, should expect to conduct prisoner security at some point during combat operations. POW security occurs in permanent areas, such as Koje-Do, or in ad hoc situations while engaging the enemy. International laws such as the Geneva Convention require sustenance, medical care, and security for POWs.[381]

Coalition commanders must consider POW security among their most significant priorities. Military forces gain a moral advantage through adherence to international law. This is particularly true if their opposing forces do not obey international law. Furthermore, complying with international law encourages a coalition's multinational

---

[379]Stairs, *The Diplomacy of Constraint: Canada, the Korean War, and the United States*, 252.

[380]Wood, *Strange Battleground: Official History of the Canadian Army in Korea*, 196.

[381]Peace Pledge Union, "Geneva Convention: An Introduction," http://www.ppu.org.uk/learn/texts/doc_geneva_con.html (accessed October 8, 2013).

governments and the populations they represent to continue their support for the coalition to continue military operations. From a Western perspective of morality, caring for POWs is simply the humane thing to do.

Perhaps the greatest lesson to be learned from Clarke's mishap is a reminder that personalities are "as important as policies" to retaining coalition unity.[382] Dwight D. Eisenhower's personality, rather than his military acumen, likely motivated his appointment as Supreme Commander of Anglo-American forces during World War II. Eisenhower's personality engendered trust from his colleagues. Conversely, Dean Acheson's personality provoked a response opposite from Eisenhower's personality. Acheson's efforts to secure Commonwealth contributions to Korea were frequently harsh. His conduct created conditions, demonstrated by Canadian protests over the employment of its troops in a POW camp, which appeared to utilize personality differences to justify policy disagreements.

Previous chapters referenced Commonwealth governments' discomfort with MacArthur's public statements and their subsequently positive attitudes towards Ridgway. Political uncertainty towards MacArthur also applied to Commonwealth soldiers. Jack Gallaway, for example, revealed this parallel between soldier and government. Gallaway fought with the RAR as a platoon sergeant. He cynically questioned if anyone would challenge MacArthur while the "living legend"[383] remained in command of UN forces. Gallaway subsequently professed great faith in Ridgway after

---

[382]Blaxland, "The Korean War: Reflections on Shared Australian and Canadian Military Experiences," 31.

[383]Gallaway, *The Last Call of the Bugle: The Long Road to Kapyong*, 170.

his assumption of command of EUSA, arguing that Ridgway turned the entire UN Command into a truly "cohesive force."[384] However, the commander cannot retain this burden alone.

All military members that represent a coalition's lead nation are required to gain the trust and confidence of their multinational partners. Lead nation military forces stimulate trust and confidence from their coalition partners through battlefield competence and a sensible decision-making methodology. Unfortunately, that which makes sense to an American, specifically in the Korean War example, is not always sensible to a non-American. Thus, Commonwealth leaders felt that American commanders in Korea failed to identify Commonwealth forces "as other than American forces."[385] America's Commonwealth partners resisted this identification and sought means to employ their forces in a manner more suitable to their capabilities than those of their "big uncle's."[386]

Commonwealth soldiers understood that the nature of combat in the Korean War changed in 1951-1952. Furthermore, following the Truman administration's policy change in search of a negotiated settlement, Commonwealth soldiers recognized that the UN Command shared parity with its Chinese enemy. With this perspective in mind, Commonwealth soldiers also assumed that the UN command could not overcome China's

---

[384]Ibid., 171.

[385]Stairs, *The Diplomacy of Constraint: Canada, the Korean War, and the United States*, 205.

[386]Blaxland, "The Korean War: Reflections on Shared Australian and Canadian Military Experiences," 32-33.

ability to provide personnel to its military forces. Thus, Commonwealth soldiers came to believe that China could not be defeated in Korea's Northern provinces.[387]

The UN Command needed "substantial reinforcement" at the selected point of attack and a "willingness to accept very heavy casualties" to achieve battlefield success after the Chinese invasion.[388] Commonwealth formations felt that tactics of this nature were the only means possible to break the Korean stalemate and achieve favorable conditions for an armistice. Commonwealth leaders clearly did not believe in the UN Command's potential to achieve a decisive victory or unify Korea. Evidence suggests that the Commonwealth, specifically the British and Australians, were prepared to do their part to maintain the status quo antebellum as long as American commanders avoided acts that were "in defiance of all common sense."[389]

From a military perspective, the Korean War provides five strong lessons. First, coalition forces should not engage in combat unless they are prepared for combat. General Walker, for example, wanted to establish 2 PPCLI near the front line immediately after it arrived to Korea. 2 PPCLI's minimal preparation for combat forced its commander, Lieutenant-Colonel Stone, to utilize his government's orders mandating a period of collective training to justify his request for such a training period to Walker. Stone's actions undoubtedly saved Canadian, and other coalition, lives.

---

[387]Farrar-Hockley, *The British Part in the Korean War, Volume I: A Distant Obligation*, 350.

[388]Johnston, *A War of Patrols: Canadian Army Operations in Korea*, 162.

[389]Gallaway, *The Last Call of the Bugle: The Long Road to Kapyong*, 169.

Secondly, military organizations must be thoroughly prepared prior to deploying to the combat theater. Subordinate commanders cannot expect understanding and compromise from the coalition commander in a manner similar to Walker if they already arrived to the combat area. Military commanders continuously seek to increase their available resources, specifically personnel, to accomplish their mission. An unprepared military organization that arrives to the combat theater is of no use to the coalition commander. This situation will breed contempt between the coalition commander and their subordinate multinational commander. This contempt is likely to spread to political levels, specifically to respective national governments. Unity amongst military echelons is hard to achieve if political leaders are not united.

Third, commanders are likely to prioritize their national policies over the coalition commander's directives. Commanders will always work to accomplish their assigned missions. However, they will perform this task under restrictions placed on them by their respective national government. Coalition commanders must understand their partners, remain patient, and respect individual nations' caveats. St Laurent's government, for example, wanted Canadian military forces sent to Korea to retain as much independence as possible to ensure Canada's position at the negotiating table. Canada's military commanders, therefore, pursued means to retain their independence from American and other Commonwealth commanders in Korea.

Fourth, national governments contributing forces must achieve shared understanding of the coalition's timeline, tasks, and purpose with the lead nation. 2 PPCLI, for example, left North America believing that it would perform occupation duties after arriving to Korea. Combat circumstances in Korea clearly favored the UN

142

Command when 2 PPCLI departed for Korea in November 1950. The Chinese invasion changed the circumstances. Unfortunately, Acheson's demands for land forces hastened Canada's deployment of untrained forces to Korea.

Canadian haste created 2 PPCLI's poor level of preparation at its departure. However, Acheson and his Canadian counterpart, Lester Pearson, should have reached an understanding of expectations for the employment of Canadian forces before their deployment. Subsequently, Acheson and Pearson should have reached an understanding of when those forces would actually be prepared to engage enemy forces in combat. Acheson's lack of patience and respect forced 2 PPCLI's hasty deployment to Korea and, therefore, negatively affected political and military relations between the United States and Canada.

Finally, coalition forces must gain and maintain trust and confidence in each other and, specifically, in the lead nation's military forces. Commonwealth perceptions of American military units "bugging out"[390] when faced with Chinese assaults did not provoke Commonwealth trust or confidence in their American partners. Additionally, lead nation military actions such as unorganized retreats prompt coalition partners to question the lead nation's competence and overall resolve to accomplish the coalition's mission. Furthermore, "fool-hardy stunts"[391] which do not serve a military purpose are not a means to gain a subordinate's trust and confidence.

---

[390]Trembath, *A Different Sort of War: Australians in Korea 1950-53*, 136.

[391]Blaxland, "The Korean War: Reflections on Shared Australian and Canadian Military Experiences," 30.

In conclusion, a coalition's military component affects the organization's ability to achieve unity of effort with greater influence than its political component. Political leaders determine the coalition's purpose and end state, decide to contribute forces, and apply respective national caveats to their forces to achieve respective national goals. However, military leaders are required to turn political guidance into battlefield success. Military considerations vis-à-vis the Korean War demonstrated that unity of effort is a critical element that supports a coalition's efforts to accomplish its mission. Specifically, the Korean War's military considerations demonstrated the important weight that personalities and relationships hold on coalition unity. Dominance in personnel and materiél does not justify attempts by a lead nation's military representative to enforce their will on a coalition partner. One must ensure their forces are sufficiently credible to support their demands of coalition partners if they find it necessary to act in such a manner. Otherwise, perceptions of military ineptitude by the lead nation will reduce coalition unity.

CHAPTER 5

COALITION SUSTAINMENT PART II

Negotiations, Repatriation, a Fixated Ally,
and the Korean Armistice

The Canadian view, shared by Great Britain and to a lesser extent Australia, was
that the United Nations lacked the means of imposing any solution upon the
Communist representatives which they were unwilling to accept voluntarily.
— Denis Stairs, *The Diplomacy of Constraint: Canada,
the Korean War, and the United States*

Armistice negotiations, POW repatriation, and UN difficulties with ROK

President Rhee Syngman are the Korean War's predominant themes from late 1951 until

1953. Negotiations for an armistice to the Korean War consumed nearly two years.

United States President Harry S. Truman received substantial blame for the negotiations'

longevity for his insistence on voluntary POW repatriation. However, representatives

from China, the DPRK, and Rhee Syngman must also receive their share of blame.

Relations between the United States and its British Commonwealth partners continued to

decline, regardless of blame ownership, in the course of negotiations to end the Korean

War.

Negotiations to end the Korean War began on July 8, 1951.[392] General Matthew

Ridgway, the commander of UN forces, announced his command's intentions to meet

with Chinese and DPRK military leaders for "talks concerning cessation of military

---

[392]Jonathan M. House, *A Military History of the Cold War, 1944-1962* (Norman:
University of Oklahoma Press, 2012), 206.

activities and establishment of peace."[393] The Truman administration selected Ridgway to initiate negotiations for two reasons. First, the United States did not diplomatically recognize the People's Republic of China (PRC) or the DPRK. Second, the Truman administration wanted a UN military representative to negotiate with enemy military leaders because those leaders were supposedly "volunteers."[394]

The Truman administration's position on negotiating with China's political leadership is sensible from a solely American perspective. United States negotiators could not discuss armistice points with agents from regimes unrecognized by their own government. Additionally, Chinese soldiers in Korea could not officially represent the PRC if they fought in Korea as an unsanctioned, or "volunteer," force. Therefore, it was sensible for American military leaders to negotiate with military leaders from China's volunteer force.

However, the Truman administration's position ignored three critical facts. First, the administration ignored the fact that negotiations to end a war are an extension of that conflict rather than a separate entity. Thus, political representatives should have been included in the UN Command's negotiating team. Second, the Truman administration's initial position on armistice negotiations discounted the perspectives of its coalition partners. Specifically, some of its partners maintained diplomatic relations with China and, therefore, maintained more than a passing interest in armistice discussions. Finally,

---

[393]Truman, *Memoirs by Harry S. Truman. Volume Two: Years of Trial and Hope*, 459.

[394]Acheson, *The Korean War*, 121.

146

the Truman administration's desire to negotiate an armistice for the Korean War with military personnel ignored the PRC government's new status as an Asian power.

Britain, a critical United States partner in Korea, was an American partner that recognized China's communist government.[395] This thesis previously cited the desire of Clement Attlee's government to protect Britain's commercial interests in China and Hong Kong as its justification for this recognition. Evidence does not suggest that subsequent operations in Korea, specifically after the Chinese invasion, reduced Attlee's desire. Conversely, it is likely that his desire to protect Britain's commerce increased, particularly after China invaded Korea and made war against a coalition that included British military units. The Truman administration wrongly overlooked this consideration.

Truman's administration also disregarded reality. Zhou Enlai, China's Premier, publicly identified the United States as China's "most dangerous enemy" in September 1950.[396] Additionally, Zhou sent messages to the Truman administration through intermediaries to warn that China would not remain idle if the UN Command advanced into the DPRK with non-ROK forces.[397] Therefore, the Chinese government, recently established 1949, could not appear weak domestically or internationally by allowing the UN Command to move unimpeded to its borders. The Chinese government's position and intent appeared clear to everyone except Truman's administration. The PRC

---

[395]Dockrill, "The Foreign Office, Anglo-American Relations and the Korean War, June 1950-June 1951," 459.

[396]U.S. Department of State, Foreign Policy Studies Branch, Chronology of Principle Events Relating to the Korean Conflict, September 1950, 30.

[397]U.S. Department of State, Foreign Policy Studies Branch, Chronology of Principle Events Relating to the Korean Conflict, October 1950, ii.

unquestionably sanctioned the "volunteer" force to engage the UN Command in combat operations. Militaries in communist nations do not initiate activity independently without receiving orders from their government. China's volunteer force forced a complete UN withdrawal from North Korea. This withdrawal initially caused Truman's administration to consider a total withdrawal of all UN force from Korea.[398] Subsequently, China presented itself as America's military equal by battling to a stalemate in Korea. Therefore, the PRC's political leaders rightly deserved to participate in armistice negotiations. Truman's administration was wrong to pursue an armistice through military negotiators alone.

Three possible reasons exist to suggest the Truman administration's reasons for ignoring China's political leaders as it pursued an armistice. First, Truman and his administration maintained a severe hatred of communism. Second, Truman's administration believed that the Chinese government was a mere satellite of the Soviet Union. Racist attitudes towards the Chinese also exist as a possible third reason. All three reasons exist as credible explanations for the Truman administration's refusal to negotiate with the Chinese government.

The first two reasons are related. Truman's personal view that communism represented "the outrage of brainwashing"[399] likely slanted his view of China's government. Therefore, it is unlikely that Truman would want to negotiate with a government that did not respect human dignity. Similarly, the Soviet Union was

[398]Morton H. Halperin, "The Limiting Process of the Korean War," *Political Science Quarterly* 78, no. 1 (March 1963): 19.

[399]Truman, *Memoirs by Harry S. Truman. Volume Two: Years of Trial and Hope*, 269.

American's primary enemy. The Truman administration already believed that Soviets authorized and sponsored the DPRK's invasion of the ROK. Therefore, it was logical, though misguided, for the Truman administration to believe that China's government blindly operated under the orders of the Soviet government.

Conversely, the Truman administration appeared to disregard the Chinese because of their ethnicity. Dean Acheson, for example, considered the Chinese incompetent at civil administration simply because of their race. Specifically, he believed that China's political leaders would meet the same fate as their predecessors and fail to retain control of their government.[400] Therefore, it is possible that Truman's administration did not want to negotiate with the Chinese government because it did not believe that China's current government would retain power for a substantial period. Additionally, Truman's administration conceivably doubted the Chinese government's trustworthiness, particularly regarding its willingness to honor the armistice's agreements.

China's communist government sought two specific results from the armistice negotiations. First, it wanted all Western nations, including the United States, to recognize its position as China's legitimate government. Second, the Communist Chinese government wanted to occupy China's seat in the United Nations Security Council.[401] The Chinese government's goals are understandable, logical, and, from a distant perspective, reasonable.

---

[400]David S. McClellan, "Dean Acheson and the Korean War," *Political Science Quarterly* 83, no. 1 (March 1968): 18.

[401]Acheson, *The Korean War*, 121.

Every state wants to receive diplomatic recognition from the world's nations. This recognition aids that respective nation's economy and, furthermore, provides validation of that nation's government to its population. However, representing China in the UN Security Council was perhaps the Chinese government's greater goal. Its control of mainland China and its massive population far outweighed the Nationalist Chinese government's claim to represent all of China. Thus, from a viewpoint developed roughly sixty years after the Korean War ended, the Truman administration's refusal to allow the PRC government to represent China in the UN Security Council appears to be a wasteful effort that produced nothing but increased Sino-American antagonism.

Attlee found the Chinese government's requests reasonable given the circumstances. He identified recognition of Communist China as an "unwelcome"[402] but necessary policy and continually sought to persuade Truman to accept this reality. Attlee's efforts met continuous resistance from Truman's administration.[403] The Truman administration's pursuit of an armistice through military means rendered China's goals unobtainable in American-led negotiations. The administration's efforts to apply a "one size fits all" approach to negotiations and negotiate solely from a perspective of American considerations ignored the wishes of a foe that proved itself America's equal in war.

The Truman administration's efforts also ignored the UN Command's collective combat exhaustion. Soldiers of democratic nations will fight for an identifiable cause.

---

[402]Fitzsimmons, *The Foreign Policy of the British Labour Government 1945-1951*, 139.

[403]U.S. Department of State, Foreign Policy Studies Branch, Chronology of Principle Events Relating to the Korean Conflict, December 1950, iv.

However, the absence of such a cause reduces their willingness to make war. Thus, the Truman administration's unwavering negotiating position, by ignoring its adversary's desires, affected the UN coalition in two ways. First, its position created conditions that would prolong the war. Importantly, American and Commonwealth soldiers identified their cause as simply to return home alive. This condition continued to reduce unity within the UN Command.

Ridgway, for his part, felt that peace "might be just around the next corner"[404] when he extended an offer near the war's first anniversary to negotiate a settlement to end the Korean War. Unfortunately, the UN Command and Chinese forces consumed five months after Ridgway's initial offer to negotiate a truce line, or a demarcation zone to remain uncrossed by any force, in Korea before commencing negotiations.[405] The delay in beginning negotiations forecasted the struggles to arise during their conduct.

Ridgway and Chinese military representatives initially agreed to negotiate at Kaesong. This location existed in a zone identified by both parties as neutral. UN representatives arrived at the location and found it surrounded by Chinese forces. According to Truman's administration, Chinese forces, attempting to intimidate UN negotiators, violated the site's neutrality.[406] Conversely, Chinese representatives argued

---

[404]Ridgway, *The Korean War*, 183.

[405]Blair, *The Forgotten War: America in Korea 1950-53*, 960.

[406]Acheson, *The Korean War*, 125.

that the UN Command violated the site's neutrality and suspended negotiations on August 23, 1951.[407]

UN-Chinese disputes regarding Kaesong's neutrality violations demonstrated that armistice negotiations would be neither seamless nor fast. The fault for the negotiation delays, however, is debatable. China's justification for surrounding the negotiating site is unknown. It is probable that its military leaders wanted to intimidate UN negotiators. It is also believable that China's leadership, either political or military, felt frustrated by American inflexibility and blamed the United States for the five months required to determine the negotiating site. Certainly, the Chinese scheme did not improve the Truman administration's perspective of China's culture or its soldiers. Unfortunately, this action likely only increased Truman's resolve to concede nothing to the Chinese.

Truman strongly believed in the UN's negotiating strength. He felt the UN Command unquestionably defeated the communist threat when negotiations began.[408] This belief persuaded UN negotiators to negotiate from a position that identified compromise with the communist enemy as unacceptable.[409] Ridgway supported this approach. He argued that any UN concession to the enemy signaled weakness that would encourage further communist military operations and delays at the negotiating table.[410]

---

[407]O'Neill, *Australia in the Korean War 1950-53. Volume I: Strategy and Diplomacy*, 509.

[408]Astor, *Presidents at War: From Truman to Bush, the Gathering of Military Power to Our Commanders in Chief*, 47.

[409]Stairs, *The Diplomacy of Constraint: Canada, the Korean War, and the United States*, 287.

[410]Blair, *The Forgotten War: America in Korea 1950-53*, 950.

Ridgway reinforced this conclusion by observing that UN forces stopped armed aggression and removed the invader from the ROK.[411]

Unfortunately, Truman and Ridgway's observations only applied to North Korea's army. The UN Command militarily dominated North Korean forces. UN forces did not militarily dominate Chinese forces. From a Commonwealth perspective, China was a "deadly opponent"[412] that definitively proved its nation's resolve to defend its borders. Clearly, Truman and Ridgway did not share the Commonwealth viewpoint. American attitudes, therefore, appear to represent the primary reason for the five months consumed to initiate armistice negotiations. However, the Communist negotiators cannot remain completely innocent.

Ridgway argued that Communist mediators negotiated by trying to wear down UN representatives through "endless and pointless argument."[413] Truman felt an "expert chess player" was necessary to comprehend communist negotiating tactics.[414] Australian historian Robert O'Neill supports these arguments. O'Neill identified the Communist Chinese as "exasperating negotiators."[415] However, O'Neill also argued that communist negotiating tactics were never sufficient to allow the UN Command to suspend armistice negotiations without incurring a moral blow.

---

[411]Ridgway, *The Korean War*, 238.

[412]Watson, *Far Eastern Tour: The Canadian Infantry in Korea, 1950-1953*, 93.

[413]Ridgway, *The Korean War*, 182.

[414]Truman, *Memoirs by Harry S. Truman. Volume Two: Years of Trial and Hope*, 89.

[415]O'Neill, *Australia in the Korean War 1950-53. Volume I: Strategy and Diplomacy*, 266.

This reality presented UN negotiators with two problems. First, they had to achieve a negotiated settlement. Suspending negotiations would allow the communist propaganda machine to portray UN culpability for prolonged negotiations to the world. This image, therefore, would increase tensions within the coalition and depict the United States as unfairly attempting to enforce its will.

Secondly, the UN Command maintained one alternative to negotiating an armistice. That option was to continue combat operations. Unfortunately, the UN Command could not unify Korea. Protracted combat operations would merely increase casualties while both sides sought to achieve meager advantages. Furthermore, domestic American opinion would not accept an increasing casualty rate because its negotiators refused to negotiate due to simple frustration. Similarly, the Commonwealth governments rightfully expected the UN coalition's lead nation to do everything in its power to negotiate an end to the Korean War while keeping casualty levels to a reasonable level. American negotiators, thus, had to negotiate regardless of Communist negotiating tactics.

Truman, Ridgway, O'Neill, and American envoys ignored Chinese culture during the armistice negotiations. Historically, the Chinese placed "heavy emphasis on strategy and stratagems."[416] Therefore, utilizing schemes and ploys, rather than specific and direct points, is a traditional component of Chinese military action and diplomacy. Furthermore, China traditionally views all aspects of war, including its aftermath, "as integral parts of

---

[416]David Lai, "Learning from the Stones: A *GO* Approach To Mastering China's Strategic Concept, *Shi*" (Monograph, U.S. Army War College, Strategic Studies Institute Carlisle PA, 2004), http://www.strategicstudiesinstitute.army.mil/pubs/display.cfm? pubID=378 (accessed October 15, 2013), 3.

the art of war."[417] Therefore, Chinese negotiators seeking to end the Korean War viewed armistice negotiations as an extension of the war rather than as a separate entity. United States negotiators, in their cultural tradition, viewed negotiations as separate from war and utilized a direct approach to discussions. Their mistakes, caused by an ignorance of Chinese culture, increased their frustration with their Chinese counterparts.

The enemy's perspectives and desires cannot remain ignored in war. American military personnel received substantial presentations on national, local, and tribal cultures to support their deployments in support of Operations Desert Shield/Desert Storm, Enduring Freedom, and Iraqi Freedom. They received these presentations to gain a greater understanding of the people they were to secure and support. However, these briefings only discussed the host nation's population. The host nation's population is not the enemy.

Respect for the enemy's culture is critical when a coalition's political or military leaders seek to negotiate an end to a conflict. At minimum, one must understand that the enemy has a culture and will act according to its maxims. One must understand their opponent's goals for the conflict and for post-conflict negotiations. These understandings help identify the opposition's negotiating tactics and style. A greater comprehension of Chinese culture, which links war and negotiations, could have prepared American negotiators to respond to their adversary's tactics. This comprehension could have reduced the protracted nature of the negotiations and saved lives while more quickly ending the war. Unfortunately, American ignorance added to the tension produced by each side's demands and prolonged efforts to reach an armistice.

---

[417]Ibid.

Casualty levels represented the significance of these misunderstandings to the UN

soldiers fighting on the ground. The five months spent haggling over a truce line, for

example, produced 60,000 UN Command casualties. Americans comprised 20,000 of

those casualties.[418] This fact should not infer that Americans fought with less intellect or

greater ferocity than their Commonwealth counterparts did. The United States

contributed more personnel to the war in Korea than its Commonwealth partners.

Therefore, one can reasonably assume that the United States incurred more casualties in

comparison to the Commonwealth.

Regardless, one can reasonably conclude that all soldiers in Korea felt frustrated

by a perceived lack of negotiating progress as their counterparts died or were injured

while delegates sought to "save face"[419] for their respective governments. This

perception likely affected their competence on the battlefield.

A small number of Canadian soldiers became "psychological casualties" due to

the war's unforeseeable conclusion.[420] Psychological casualties sought means to extricate

themselves from the battlefield for reasons other than enemy-inflicted wounds. It is

debatable if this concern existed, as well as the determination to continue fighting,

throughout the entire Commonwealth formation. Anthony Farrar-Hockley, a British

officer in Korea, argued that soldier support for the war and, thus, their desire to make

---

[418]Blair, *The Forgotten War: America in Korea 1950-53*, 960.

[419]Trembath, *A Different Sort of War: Australians in Korea 1950-53*, 143.

[420]Watson, *Far Eastern Tour: The Canadian Infantry in Korea, 1950-1953*, 93.

war reduced as negotiations continued.[421] Conversely, Jeffrey Grey, an Australian historian, considers Farrar-Hockley's observation to be a "blanket characterization."[422]

Psychological casualties are not atypical in war. Eventually, some soldiers will reach a point when they believe a trip to the hospital is more acceptable than life on the front line. This is true even when the war supports an identifiable cause. General George S. Patton, for example, famously slapped two soldiers for becoming psychological casualties during the Second World War. It is the military leader's responsibility to negate these possibilities.

Grey's assessment of the general nature of Farrar-Hockley's observation appears correct. However, prolonged armistice negotiations that did not appear to accomplish anything created conditions that made further psychological casualties in the Korean War almost understandable. Therefore, Korean War negotiations increased military leaders' responsibilities to reduce the potential for their soldiers to become psychological casualties to a degree greater than that which is considered normal. Furthermore, aggressive Chinese tactics increased these strains.

Chinese military forces appear more aggressive tactically than their UN counterparts after armistice negotiations commenced. This perception may exist because Chinese "volunteers" believed they fought in "in 'defense' of the Fatherland."[423] Conversely, UN soldiers found themselves several thousand miles away from their homes

---

[421]Farrar-Hockley, *The British Part in the Korean War, Volume I: A Distant Obligation*, 366.

[422]Grey, *The Commonwealth Armies and the Korean War. An Alliance Study*, 153.

[423]Hanson W. Baldwin, "China as a Military Power," *Foreign Affairs* 30, no. 1 (October 1951): 51.

in a "primitive and brutal" society whose soldiers appeared "more than happy" to leave the fighting to others."[424] Therefore, Chinese forces, fighting for a cause in which they seemed to believe, possessed mental and moral advantages over their enemy. They used this advantage to maintain strong pressure on American and Commonwealth formations as armistice negotiations continued.

Canadian formations, on the other hand, found their efforts to respond strongly to Chinese operations almost negligible. Major W.H. Pope, a 25th Canadian Brigade staff officer, felt his organization too frequently withdrew its patrols to static positions. Furthermore, Pope found that his organization's patrol orders sent formations that were "never strong enough to defeat the enemy"[425] into battle. Conversely, Chinese formations exhibited psychological and tactical preferences for night attacks to "instill terror" on their enemy.[426]

Chinese tactics reflected the Chinese view of negotiations as an extension of war rather than as an entity separate from war. Thus, the Chinese continued aggressive operations while officials pursued an armistice. Prolonged negotiations, at least partially caused by American ignorance of Chinese culture, increased casualties and affected the UN Command's morale and battlefield performance. This became severely problematic because Commonwealth formations logically felt that American efforts to dominate armistice negotiations were useless given their perceptions of China's military strength.

---

[424]Watson, *Far Eastern Tour: The Canadian Infantry in Korea, 1950-1953*, 60-61.

[425]Ibid., 94.

[426]Baldwin, "China as a Military Power," 59.

Such perspectives do not help soldiers accomplish their mission, let alone routine tasks. Conversely, this perception tempts soldiers and leaders to remain in stationary positions and rarely attempt to seek out and destroy the enemy.

The tendency to avoid combat is understandable given the circumstances the Commonwealth soldiers faced in Korea. Commonwealth soldiers understood that the Chinese could not be defeated. Their perspective, thus, inferred Commonwealth suppositions that the UN Command could not unify Korea. Ridgway went so far as to delay major operations to "wait and see how armistice negotiations turned out."[427] Therefore, from a Commonwealth perspective, attempts to seize a few feet or yards of ground meant nothing to armistice negotiations. These actions would only increase casualties. This perspective becomes more understandable if one considers that armistice terms were likely to force leaders to surrender battlefield gains. Unfortunately, this battlefield stalemate affected domestic American opinion and further decreased the UN coalition's unity.

Domestic American criticism of Commonwealth contributions and capabilities increased around the time initial negotiations began. The stalemate in Korea partially explains this increase. However, the MacArthur hearings more fully explain this rise in American criticism of the Commonwealth. The United States Congress held the hearings after Truman dismissed General of the Army Douglas MacArthur from command of UN forces. MacArthur's comments during the hearings encouraged American public opinion

---

[427]Ridgway, *The Korean War*, 187.

to believe that the Commonwealth's military contributions to Korea were ineffective and insufficient.[428]

Combined, the Korean stalemate and MacArthur's comments stimulated a popular American opinion that the United States was operating independently in Korea. Thus, according to American domestic opinion, the Commonwealth nations needed to contribute more land forces to the UN Command. This increase, therefore, could break the Korean stalemate and win the war. The Commonwealth, according to American opinion, simply needed to fulfill its obligations.

American opinion ignored the Commonwealth's limitations. Britain, for example, had its meager military resources dispersed in Korea, Hong Kong, Malaya, the Middle East, Austria, and Germany.[429] Australia's commitments to Middle Eastern security reduced its ability to send more than two battalions to Korea.[430] American public comments, therefore, developed within the Commonwealth governments and military formations confusion as to why their contributions and limitations remained unappreciated in the United States. Thus, the MacArthur hearings, the military stalemate, and protracted negotiations further divided the UN coalition's overall unity. Unfortunately, the subject of POW repatriation increased the protracted nature of the armistice negotiations and, thus, further diminished coalition unity.

---

[428]O'Neill, *Australia in the Korean War 1950-53*, 249.

[429]Anthony Eden, "Britain in World Strategy," *Foreign Affairs* 29, no. 3 (April 1951): 342.

[430]Jeffrey Grey, "The Formation of the Commonwealth Division, 1950-1951," *Military Affairs* 51, no. 1 (January 1987): 12.

The UN Command proposed in January 1952 that every prisoner of war retain the choice to determine whether they would return to their home country after the Korean War.[431] This proposal initially received significant support from the Commonwealth nations. Winston Churchill, elected as Britain's Prime Minister in 1952, felt that repatriation should remain voluntary.[432] Lester Pearson, Canada's Minister for External Affairs, went further by suggesting that to force communist POW to return to China or the DPRK was "unthinkable."[433]

Initial coalition reactions to the UN Command's proposal indicate levels of agreement and unity not seen within the Command, politically or militarily, since the UN first resolved to defend South Korea. Truman, Churchill, and Pearson may have disagreed on the conduct of the Korean War and other matters of world affairs. However, they all shared a similar contempt for communism and communist governments. Unfortunately, repatriation became a topic that splintered coalition unity. It is necessary to understand why this occurred if the topic received such substantial support after its initial introduction. The responsibility for this rests with Chinese and North Korean negotiators and Harry Truman.

---

[431]House, *A Military History of the Cold War, 1944-1962*, 206.

[432]Lowe, "The Significance of the Korean War in Anglo-American Relations, 1950-53," 135.

[433]Stairs, *The Diplomacy of Constraint: Canada, the Korean War, and the United States*, 245.

Negotiators from China and North Korea were initially responsive to the suggestion of voluntary repatriation.[434] This is logical. The communists believed in their system. Political commissars attached to military units ensured that those units' soldiers remained loyal to their communist governments. Therefore, one can reasonably assume that the Chinese and North Korean governments believed their POW would readily agree to return voluntarily to their homelands. However, these nations found themselves in an unpredicted situation.

The UN Command announced that 60 percent of its enemy prisoners wished to return to China or the DPRK.[435] Thus, roughly 70,000 out of approximately 116,000 Communist POW wanted to return home.[436] These figures indicated that communist propaganda was not as effective as the Chinese and North Korean governments assumed. Additionally, these figures inferred that the new regimes in China and North Korea had yet to consolidate fully their power within their respective countries.

These figures undoubtedly shocked Chinese and North Korean negotiators. One can assume that both governments wanted to expand their communist regimes, China throughout Asia and North Korea throughout the Korean peninsula. However, the preponderance of communist POW desiring voluntary repatriation indicated that the communist "struggle" to spread its ideology in the world would be harder than Chinese or

---

[434]Burton I. Kaufman, review of *A Substitute for Victory: The Politics of Peacemaking at the Korean Armistice Talks,* by Rosemary Foot, *Reviews in American History* 20, no. 4 (December 1992): 565.

[435]O'Neill, *Australia in the Korean War 1950-53. Volume I: Strategy and Diplomacy,* 511.

[436]Kaufman, review of *A Substitute for Victory: The Politics of Peacemaking at the Korean Armistice Talks,* 565.

North Korean leaders initially assumed. Furthermore, the number of communist POW that did not wish to return to their native lands justified Truman's proposal in support of voluntary repatriation. Regardless, the subject of repatriation became a significant obstacle to armistice negotiations.

Truman did not help reduce this obstacle. He insisted that voluntary repatriation was a topic on which the UN Command could not surrender. Evidence suggests that Truman would rather concede everything, even an independent North Korea, than "buy an armistice"[437] by forcibly requiring human beings to return to communist governments. Unfortunately, Truman's persistence on this issue, partially inspired by the communist's refusal to accept it, caused the UN Command to move from an initial position that advocated voluntary repatriation to a position of "no forced repatriation."[438] Specifically, this new stance sought to avoid repatriating POW with armed force. This change caused armistice negotiations to continue from January 1952, when UN negotiators first proposed the topic of repatriation, until negotiators signed the armistice. Negotiations dragged on for nearly two years because of this point.

It is necessary, before placing the majority of blame on Truman, to comment on the recent history of prisoner of war repatriation prior to the Korean War. This history shaped Truman's position on the subject. The Hague Convention of 1907 concluded that

---

[437]Truman, *Memoirs by Harry S. Truman. Volume Two: Years of Trial and Hope*, 460.

[438]Jan P. Charmatz and Harold M. Wit, "Repatriation of Prisoners of War and the 1949 Geneva Convention," *The Yale Law Journal* 62, no. 3 (February 1953): 391.

repatriation "shall be carried out as rapidly as possible" after a war's conclusion.[439] Truman's administration adhered to this policy after World War II. However, Truman soon regretted this observance.

The Soviet Union insisted on the return of all of its POW after the Second World War. A substantial number of Soviet POW attempted to avoid forced repatriation. Some attempted suicide as a means to avoid returning to the Soviet Union.[440] Additionally, American soldiers frequently had to use tear gas or other forcible means to put Soviet prisoners of war, typically captured in German military uniforms, onto trains headed for the Soviet Union. Those personnel did not wish to return to a life of "slaughter or slavery"[441] in their home country. Thus, Truman came to believe that American adherence to forced repatriation during World War II violated "the fundamental humanitarian principles we espoused."[442] Truman's administration, therefore, firmly opposed the policy of forced repatriation by 1947.[443]

Truman used experience to guide his thoughts in Korea. He likely believed that a substantial number of Chinese or North Korean prisoners wished to avoid the same fate

---

[439]Waldemar A. Sof, review of *Release and Repatriation of Prisoners of War at the End of Active Hostilities. A Study of Article 118, Paragraph 1 of the Third Geneva Convention Relative to the Treatment of Prisoners of War*," by Christian S. Delessert, *The American Journal of International Law* 72, no. 2 (April 1978): 429.

[440]Mark Elliott, "The United States and Forced Repatriation of Soviet Citizens, 1944-47," *Political Science Quarterly* 88, no. 2 (June 1973): 253.

[441]Blair, *The Forgotten War: American in Korea 1950-53*, 963.

[442]Dwight D. Eisenhower, *Crusade in Europe* (New York: Doubleday & Company, 1948), 439.

[443]Elliott, "The United States and Forced Repatriation of Soviet Citizens, 1944-47," 271.

as their Soviet predecessors. The data provided by the UN Command regarding POW who wished to return to China or North Korea demonstrated that his belief was not pure speculation. Thus, Truman's firm stance on the issue of repatriation was logical on humanitarian grounds. In this example, he correctly remained steadfast in arguing that Korean War POW should choose their final location after the war.

Unfortunately, international laws presented a legitimate roadblock to Truman's goals. Article 118 of the Geneva Prisoners of War Convention of 1949 mandated prisoner of war repatriation "without delay after the cessation of active hostilities."[444] Therefore, Truman's dogged insistence on voluntary repatriation portrayed him as attempting to "score Cold War debating points."[445] It also forced Winston Churchill, a strong promoter of Anglo-American unity, to criticize Truman's policy.[446]

The perception that Truman, or any political leader, wanted to achieve an insignificant ideological victory will not convince the governments and soldiers that represent his coalition partners to follow blindly their coalition's leadership. This idea is true regardless of the era. Governments and soldiers from democratic societies will make war for a just cause. They can maintain that unity as long as the cause remains just. However, one can easily interpret a perception as reality.

---

[444]Sof, review of *Release and Repatriation of Prisoners of War at the End of Active Hostilities*, 430.

[445]Herring, *From Colony to Superpower: U.S. Foreign Relations since 1776*, 644-45.

[446]Lowe, "The Significance of the Korean War in Anglo-American Relations, 1950-53," 133.

One can infer that Commonwealth soldiers perceived that Truman sought a psychological victory through his stance on repatriation. Furthermore, one can conclude that Commonwealth soldiers found this goal pointless and, thus, put their lives at risk. This soldier-based perspective is concerning because it likely increased Commonwealth soldiers' resentment towards the United States.

Specifically, Truman's position on repatriation raised questions from the UN Command's soldiers that wondered why they should die or suffer to give their enemies "freedom of choice over repatriation."[447] Churchill's criticism demonstrates that this perspective increased dissension throughout the entire UN Command, at political and military levels, and reduced the coalition's unity. Therefore, it is logical to conclude that this perception increased the Chinese and DPRK negotiators' desire to obtain their critical points in the armistice negotiations and their willingness to prolong armistice negotiations to achieve those demands.

Humanitarian concerns rather than a psychological victory appear to have dominated Truman's thinking on POW repatriation. This conclusion derives from American experiences with Soviet POWs after the Second World War. However, soldiers do not want to place themselves in harm's way for a perceived moral victory. The UN Command's leadership felt its primary mission, restoring the ROK's sovereignty, was completed. Nonetheless, it still needed its forces to continue combat operations as necessary. At minimum, military forces needed to conduct short-range patrols to protect their static positions from enemy artillery and direct fires.

---

[447]Blair, *The Forgotten War: America in Korea 1950-53*, 964.

A coalition without unity is a coalition that cannot accomplish its mission. Truman's position on POW repatriation reduced the UN Command's unity of effort. It reduced the willingness and ability of the Command's soldiers to continue combat operations. Therefore, the UN Command became a force that simply maintained a defensive line and "hesitated to fight for ground."[448] This line was critical to the conduct of armistice negotiations. It prevented enemy forces from invading South Korea. However, this defensive posture will not encourage soldier morale when conducted for an inconceivable cause. Unfortunately, Truman faced other struggles in addition to criticism for his stance on repatriation.

Rhee Syngman perhaps did more to prolong armistice negotiations than Truman's position on POW repatriation. Rhee could not accept anything less than a unified Korea under his rule.[449] Acheson felt Rhee's "mania for reunification" equaled Douglas MacArthur's previous desires to unify the Korean peninsula and take the war into China.[450] Rhee's desires did not conform to the goals of the UN Command in Korea and, therefore, the goals of the Truman administration. However, the Truman administration could not simply force Rhee to adhere blindly to its policies.

Rhee was South Korea's president. Therefore, Truman's administration and the UN Command could not ignore outright Rhee's objectives. His status as a difficult ally finds a parallel in America's frustration with Afghanistan President Hamid Karzai during

---

[448]Ridgway, *The Korean War*, 187.

[449]Truman, *Memoirs by Harry S. Truman. Volume Two: Years of Trial and Hope*, 462.

[450]Acheson, *The Korean War*, 125.

Operation Enduring Freedom. As the political leaders of their respective states, Rhee and Karzai possessed the option to act independent of United States wishes. Rhee obstructed the progress of armistice negotiations during the Korean War. Karzai's refusal to include the Taliban in negotiations to end the war in Afghanistan presented American officials with similar frustrations.

Rhee and Karzai understood that their nations relied on the United States to protect their young regimes. Regardless, each man's reliance on American financial and military support did not prevent him from publicly stating personal opinions that contrasted with American policy. However, perceptions of the relationship between Korean or Afghan reliance on American assistance and their subservience to American goals neglect a critical point. Specifically, they ignore the support Rhee and Karzai maintained within their respective countries and the process that brought them to their positions.

Rhee controlled a strong army, was relatively popular in the ROK, and, specifically, maintained the loyalty of key personnel within his police and civil administration.[451] Furthermore, his election occurred under the supervision of the UN. Therefore, the Truman administration could not arbitrarily remove him from power in favor of a person more agreeable to its wishes. The United States did create a plan at one point to mount a coup against Rhee.[452] Fortunately, it never executed this plan. To do so

---

[451]O'Neill, *Australia in the Korean War 1950-53. Volume I: Strategy and Diplomacy*, 358.

[452]Robert F. Futtrell, review of *The Korean War: Challenges in Crisis, Credibility, and Command*, by Burton I. Kaufman, *The Journal of American History* 73, no. 3 (December 1986): 810.

would alienate the ROK population and encourage international condemnation of the United States. Additionally, it would justify communist propaganda regarding Western concepts of superiority over Asians. American knowledge and acceptance of the South Vietnamese coup against Ngo Dinh Diem in 1963 reflected this concept.

Similarly, Karzai maintains generally strong tribal support in Afghanistan. Agreements, even discussions, with the Taliban cannot occur without his approval. Thus, Karzai's position, like Rhee's, allowed him to command the Afghan National Security Forces independent of American plans or wishes. Furthermore, both men reached their respective offices through democratic means.

A forced removal of Karzai as President of Afghanistan, regardless of its potential desirability, cannot occur without severe backlash from the international community and tribes within Afghanistan that support him. This fact also applied to Rhee. The United States, therefore, could not simply remove the links that bound it to Rhee or Karzai and conduct independent negotiations with its respective enemies. This fact frustrated the Truman administration and its successor.

The United States elected Dwight D. Eisenhower President in 1952. More than two-thirds of the United States elected him specifically to take "strong steps" to end the Korean War.[453] This fact demonstrates the frustrations that Truman's position on prisoner repatriation produced in the United States and the Commonwealth. Eisenhower contributed to the end of the Korean War in two major areas. First, his administration suggested that it might use atomic weapons to motivate the Chinese and DPRK

---

[453]Roger Dingman, "Atomic Diplomacy During the Korean War," *International Security* 13, no. 3 (Winter 1988-1989): 81.

negotiators to agree to armistice terms.[454] Second, Eisenhower convinced Rhee to accept an armistice.

The effects of the Eisenhower administration's suggestions regarding the use of atomic bombs against China are debatable. John Foster Dulles, Eisenhower's Secretary of State, argued in 1956 that the speed at which the Chinese and DPRK negotiators agreed to an armistice after the suggested use of atomic bombs was a "pretty fair inference" that the threat worked.[455] Dulles' comment may be correct. However, it did not consider China's perspectives.

Three possibilities exist to explain China's eventual agreement to an armistice. First, it is likely that the Korean War sufficiently damaged China's economy to persuade Mao Zedong's government to agree to a solution acceptable to China. This possibility is feasible because Mao did not inherit an economic powerhouse. Given his regime's youth, it is reasonable to assume that Mao understood his requirement to consolidate fully his government and economically move China forward.

Conversely, it is conceivable that Mao's government agreed to the armistice because it felt it received "maximum political value" from the war.[456] This logic is also reasonable. The Chinese military represented itself as equal to that of the UN Command. Therefore, military success against the United States turned a young Chinese government into a world power. Extending the war beyond achieving this objective meant would cost China substantial workers necessary to invigorate its economy.

---

[454]House, *A Military History of the Cold War, 1944-1962*, 207.

[455]Dingman, "Atomic Diplomacy During the Korean War," 50.

[456]House, *A Military History of the Cold War, 1944-1962*, 208.

Finally, the DPRK lost some of its "territorial integrity"[457] due to the war. However, one again must consider Chinese history to understand the importance behind the DPRK's continued existence after 1953. Hostile nations historically used the Korean peninsula as an invasion route into China. Japan, for example, invaded Korea in 1592 with intentions to conquer subsequently China.[458] Therefore, given that precedent, the existence of a friendly DPRK on China's border provided Mao's government with a buffer against potential invaders.

Evidence suggests that the Commonwealth governments did not strongly protest the Eisenhower administration's suggested use of atomic bombs. This is interesting when one considers the Commonwealth's collective concern after Truman suggested the possibility of using atomic bombs after the initial Chinese invasion in December 1950. The Commonwealth governments roundly criticized Truman's statement. His remark caused Attlee, concerned about Truman's intentions, to fly to Washington to confer with his coalition partner to receive Truman's assurance that he did not intend to utilize atomic weapons in Korea.

Truman and the Commonwealth's government leaders wanted to avoid an escalation of the Korean War in 1950. The Commonwealth governments felt Truman's remark threatened this goal. One can logically conclude that all governments wanted to contain the war to Korea in 1953. However, Korea's situation in 1953 was different from its situation in 1950. The war in Korea exhausted politically and militarily the United

---

[457]Halperin, "The Limiting Process of the Korean War," 19.

[458]Kenneth M. Swope, "Turning the Tide: The Strategic and Psychological Significance of the Liberation of Pyongyang in 1593," *War and Society* 21, no. 2 (October 2003): 4.

States and its Commonwealth partners. Nearly two years of armistice negotiations, prolonged by communist negotiating tactics and Truman's position on POW repatriation, appear to have forced the Commonwealth governments to accept any alternative to ending the war that Eisenhower might suggest.

Eisenhower's other major contribution to ending the Korean War, more important than his threats of atomic war, was to convince Rhee to accept an armistice to end the Korean War. Rhee, seeking a unified Korea under his government, economic assistance, and ROK inclusion in an American Pacific security agreement, tried to sway Eisenhower to his goals.[459] Eisenhower, seeking any means to end the war, wrote Rhee in June 1953 to recommend that they pursue Korean unification through "political and other methods"[460] that did not involve military forces. Rhee, replying in July 1953, promised to "cease his obstruction" of the armistice negotiations.[461] All concerned parties signed the armistice to end the Korean War on July 27, 1953.[462]

The armistice, primarily delayed by disagreements on POW repatriation, was signed three years and one month after the DPRK invaded the ROK. More than 20,000 POWs from China and the DPRK elected not to return to their homelands.[463] Nearly seventy percent of the UN Command's Chinese prisoners refused repatriation.

---

[459]O'Neill, *Australia in the Korean War 1950-53. Volume I: Strategy and Diplomacy*, 323.

[460]Ridgway, *The Korean War*, 269.

[461]O'Neill, *Australia in the Korean War 1950-53. Volume I: Strategy and Diplomacy*, 359.

[462]House, *A Military History of the Cold War, 1944-1962*, 208.

[463]Grey, *The Commonwealth Armies and the Korean War. An Alliance Study*, 183.

Communist forces took prisoner 7,140 Americans. 2,701 Americans died in captivity.[464]

Twenty-one American prisoners out of the 4,418 still living elected to remain in China or

North Korea.[465] Therefore, of those still living, less than one-half of one percent of

American POW refused repatriation to the United States. Furthermore, only one British

officer refused repatriation to Great Britain.[466] All Canadian and Australian prisoners

elected to return home.[467]

These numbers are significant for two reasons. First, the small number of UN

soldiers that refused repatriation demonstrates a major preference for life in Western

society. Therefore, the extensive number of communist POWs refusing repatriation

validated Truman's position supporting voluntary repatriation. Thus, one can perceive

that the length of the Korean War, though tragic and costly, did more than score "points"

for the United States and the UN. These numbers invalidated Communist claims to their

form of government's superiority over capitalist societies. Furthermore, Truman's

position on repatriation undoubtedly saved many Chinese and Korean lives.

Unfortunately, the war consumed thousands of casualties to confirm Truman's opinion.

---

[464]U.S. Department of Veterans Affairs, "Former American Prisoners of War (POWs)," April 2005, http://www.va.gov/vetdata/docs/SpecialReports/POWCY04Final 4-7-05forweb.pdf (accessed November 8, 2013), 3.

[465]House, *A Military History of the Cold War, 1944-1962*, 208.

[466]Ibid.

[467]Blaxland, "The Korean War: Reflections on Shared Australian and Canadian Military Experiences," 31.

The Korean War produced more casualties than any war in the twentieth century except for the two world wars.[468] The war cost the United States more than 142,000 killed, wounded, missing, or captured.[469] Its 33,000 killed in action occurred in a period of three years. In comparison, the United States suffered 58,000 casualties over a longer period during the Vietnam War.

Canadian soldiers suffered 516 deaths, of which 312 occurred on the battlefield.[470] Britain lost nearly one thousand troops to combat-related deaths. More than 300 Australian soldiers died in Korea.[471] Casualties from China and the DPRK were "likely more than a million" while the ROK lost more than 66,000 soldiers.[472]

These casualty numbers reflect a government's responsibility to determine its political goals before sending military forces into combat. This thesis does not negatively judge Truman for sending American soldiers to Korea. However, he made two critical decisions that created these high casualty numbers. First, he decided to cross the 38th Parallel to unify the Korean peninsula. Second, Truman insisted, however well intentioned, on voluntary POW repatriation. His position on POW repatriation would

---

[468]Allan R. Millett, "Introduction to the Korean War," *The Journal of Military History* 65, no. 4 (October 2001): 924.

[469]James R. Arnold, *Presidents Under Fire. Commanders in Chief in Victory and Defeat* (New York: Orion Books, 1994), 205.

[470]Melady, *Korea: Canada's Forgotten War*, 178.

[471]Trembath, *A Different Sort of War: Australians in Korea 1950-53*, 1.

[472]Blaxland, "The Korean War: Reflections on Shared Australian and Canadian Military Experiences," 31.

have held more credibility with his coalition partners and their enemy if he ordered the UN Command to stop at the 38th Parallel in October 1950.

The UN Command, at that time, was undoubtedly victorious. It defeated the North Korean army and protected South Korea. Unfortunately, Truman's ensuing decisions created a chain of events that extended the war and increased casualties on all sides. The war could have ended when the UN Command first reached the 38th Parallel. The UN Command could have demanded and received anything it wanted at that time. Truman's Commonwealth partners likely did not plan on this extension and its subsequent effects when they decided to commit military forces to the American-led coalition.

Therefore, the Korean War ended the "relatively easy and automatic political relations"[473] the United States and the Commonwealth nations enjoyed before the war. Eisenhower, upon assuming the presidency, identified that Anglo-American relations were worse "than at any time since the Second World War."[474] Australia, having gained the Pacific security pact it pursued at the start of the Korean War, appears to be the only Commonwealth member that maintained a truly positive relationship with the United States after the war.

Several factors explain the breakdown in American-Commonwealth relations. Unfortunately, this breakdown began when the DPRK invaded the ROK. Truman's administration understood that each Commonwealth nation maintained a particular

---

[473]Holmes, "Canada and the United States in World Politics," 105.

[474]Lowe, "The Significance of the Korean War in Anglo-American Relations, 1950-53," 145.

reliance on the United States. Truman administration officials, therefore, typically acted in a haughty manner towards their Commonwealth counterparts when the Korean War began. Evidence suggests that the Truman administration used its position of influence to stimulate Commonwealth governments to contribute forces to the UN coalition. The Truman administration was not wrong to seek assistance from the Commonwealth. Participation from as many UN members as possible in Korea legitimized the UN's mandate for the ROK. However, American coalition development tactics merely foreshadowed the Truman administration's conduct for the duration of the war.

The Korean War did not end the West's struggle against communism. The Cold War lasted nearly 40 years after the Korean War ended. Thus, America's post-1953 relationships with its coalition partners present the appearance that the Truman administration from 1950-1953 risked its enduring global goals to achieve short-term successes in Korea. Therefore, the Truman administration's decisions and behaviors during the Korean War established a precedent for future American presidents.

Several of Truman's successors sent the United States military to various countries during their respective terms in office. His decision to stop the expansion of communism into the ROK established a precedent for these decisions. Lyndon Johnson, for example, increased American contributions to Vietnam. Johnson, like Truman, wanted to stop the expansion of communism. It is not unreasonable to suggest that the attitude of George W. Bush's administration towards its allies and potential coalition partners followed the Truman administration's Korean example. This temperament arose after the Bush administration initiated the War on Terror. The administration's "with or against us" philosophy created conditions that sent American military forces to distant locations and offended several American allies.

Such was the case in Korea. Truman does not possess sole ownership for the war's longevity. He had to deal with an inflexible, albeit legitimate ally in Rhee Syngman. His communist enemies proved themselves wily and inflexible negotiators. However, Truman's decisions, specifically regarding his position on POW repatriation, created conditions that encouraged that longevity. His decisions created higher casualties in a war that remained heavily unsupported in its final two years. Truman's decisions increased tensions within a coalition that was already fragmented. This reduced unity in Korea affected American relations with its Commonwealth partners in all other areas of diplomacy after the war ended.

CHAPTER 6

CONCLUSIONS

Much time and effort is expended in learning about the enemy; a similar effort is required to understand the doctrine, capabilities, strategic goals, culture, religion, customs, history, and values of each partner.

— Chairman, Joint Chiefs of Staff,
Joint Publication 3-16, *Multinational Operations*

This study focused on the Truman administration's coalition development efforts concerning Great Britain, Canada, and Australia during the 1950-1953 Korean War. The study selected these members of the British Commonwealth because they were America's most critical partners prior to 1950. The United States and Great Britain held a "special relationship"[475] that dated back to the Second World War. Canada and Australia maintained common Anglo-Saxon heritage with the United States. Furthermore, Canada and the United States shared national borders and interdependent economies. Additionally, the United States and Australia shared several strategic interests in the Pacific.

Joint Publication 3-16, *Multinational Operations* provides several recommendations that are critical to this study. First, it recommends that American military forces utilize tenets such as respect and patience when interacting with their multinational partners. American military forces should apply these tenets while improving their knowledge of their partners' history, culture, and values. Additionally, JP 3-16 reminds its audience that political goals motivate a nation's decision to contribute forces to a coalition. It advises American forces to refrain from expecting automatic

---

[475]Craig, "The Political Leader as Strategist," 501.

contributions from allies. Furthermore, JP 3-16 cautions American commanders to recognize their limitations with multinational forces. Finally, JP 3-16 recommends that American leaders provide clear strategic direction to guide the coalition's operations.

Joint Publication 3-16 rightfully exists as the American military's doctrinal foundation for the conduct of coalition operations. It does not identify the 1950-1953 Korean War as a source of its content. Sixteen nations contributed to a coalition that accomplished its objective. However, JP 3-16 did not exist when President Harry S. Truman's administration developed a coalition to defend the Republic of Korea in 1950. Therefore, Truman's administration built and led its coalition with some questionable methods. Evidence demonstrates that JP 3-16 captures a majority of important lessons from the Truman administration's conduct during the Korean War. Correct applications of JP 3-16's doctrine engender multinational support for American policies and are likely to remove from the United States the burden to conduct unilateral military operations.

Joint Publication 3-16 fails to discuss five critical lessons from the Truman administration's leadership during the Korean War. First, JP 3-16 does not specifically address operations conducted to defend another country. Second, JP 3-16 does not provide guidance for situations such as a coalition member's proposal to change the coalition mission. Third, JP 3-16 does not identify the fact that soldiers from the lead nation, under whose command and control coalition members place their forces,[476] represent their nation's capability and credibility. Fourth, it does not discuss respect for enemy culture. Finally, JP 3-16 fails to review the negative effects of heavy casualties on morale.

---

[476]Chairman, Joint Chiefs of Staff, Joint Publication 3-16 (2007), xii.

The publication's omissions are relevant to future coalition operations. Specifically, JP 3-16's guidance and exclusions apply as much to political leaders as they do to military personnel. To ignore these omissions, therefore, is to risk a coalition's unity of effort at political and military levels. Truman's administration would have benefitted by having a manual such as JP 3-16 in 1950.

At the political level, the Truman administration did not always treat its Commonwealth partners with respect and patience. Minimal American knowledge of Commonwealth limitations or, more likely, a refusal to recognize them contributed to the Truman administration's harsh tactics. The Truman administration's behavior is somewhat understandable if one considers that it received "primary responsibility"[477] from the UN to execute the UN mission for Korea. However, the Truman administration's methods caused the Commonwealth nations to contribute forces for purely political, rather than moral, reasons.

Joint Publication 3-16 provides an initial source from which the United States military can learn and apply to avoid replicating American behavior during the Korean War. However, additional measures are required to ensure that American military personnel are capable of applying JP 3-16's recommendations to future operations. For example, American military personnel receive numerous, albeit insufficient, presentations on foreign cultures during their careers. Personal experience with foreign cultures is the best means for the United States military to achieve a greater understanding of American allies and potential coalition partners. The United States

---

[477]U.S. Department of State, World Reaction to Korean Developments, Special Supplement, July 18, 1950, Harry S. Truman Library, Independence, MO.

military already conducts personnel exchange programs with numerous countries. It needs to increase the scope of such programs to diversify further its personnel and create conditions that generate multinational support for United States objectives.

Increased foreign language training is another method with which to develop a military member's understanding of foreign cultures and history. Education in this form broadens the military representative and enhances their ability to apply JP 3-16's suggestions. This skill enables American personnel to provide the best representation of the United States to foreign partners. However, failure to broaden military personnel in peace will diminish their ability to interact with foreign personnel in war. Actions by the Truman administration and its military personnel within the UN Command demonstrated this argument.

Marginal respect was most evident in American interactions with British and Canadian officials. Dean Acheson, Truman's Secretary of State, and Sir Oliver Franks, Britain's ambassador to the United States, enjoyed a "close friendship" before June 1950.[478] Similarly, Truman's administration maintained good relations with Canada's Louis St Laurent government prior to June 1950. However, Acheson demanded repeatedly that Britain contribute forces to "set a good pattern"[479] for other nations.

---

[478]Dockrill, "The Foreign Office, Anglo-American Relations and the Korean War, June 1950-June 1951," 476.

[479]Memorandum of Conversation: Proposed UK Note Relating to Increased Military Effort; China, Dean Acheson and Sir Oliver Franks, August 3, 1950, 2. Papers of Dean Acheson, Harry S. Truman Library, Independence, MO.

Additionally, Acheson used language more "forceful" with Canada's Minister for

External Affairs, Lester Pearson, to gain Canadian contributions.[480]

According to JP 3-16, the tenet of respect applies to a nation's national honor and

prestige.[481] Furthermore, JP 3-16 identifies that a nation's prestige is as important as its

military capabilities and contributions. Acheson's tactics did not exhibit these

considerations. Therefore, his actions created problems in American relations with Great

Britain and Canada. American diplomatic problems with these Commonwealth members

existed for the remainder of the Korean War and into the post-war years.

This thesis does not apply present-day standards of personal diplomacy to the

standards that existed in 1950. However, Acheson's tactics were thoughtless and

disrespectful. JP 3-16's tenet of respect goes beyond merely respecting a potential

contributing nation's concerns for its national prestige. It includes respect for

representatives of coalition partners, and potential partners, as people that are responsible

for their respective nations' welfare. Acheson ignored such basic facts of diplomacy. As

the United States Secretary of State, he had a responsibility to support American

interests. He did everything possible to meet his responsibilities. However, Acheson

should also have realized that Franks and Pearson held similar responsibilities for Great

Britain and Canada.

---

[480]Memorandum of Conversation: Formosa; Contribution of Troops by Canada, Dean Acheson and Lester B. Pearson, July 29, 1950, Papers of Dean Acheson, Harry S. Truman Library, Independence, MO.

[481]Chairman, Joint Chiefs of Staff, Joint Publication 3-16 (2007), I-3.

The United States was the superpower of the non-communist world in 1950.[482]

Therefore, defending South Korea against communist aggression benefitted American

interests because it demonstrated American credibility to non-communist states.

Successfully defending the ROK aided Australian interests because it would deter future

communist aggression in Asia.

Aside from enhancing UN credibility, defending the ROK did not directly support

British or Canadian interests. Winston Churchill, for example, argued that defending

Western Europe, "not Korea," mattered to British interests.[483] Thus, Truman's

administration should have employed more civil diplomacy to gain support for a cause

with international implications.

Domestic American politics also explains the behavior of American officials such

as Acheson. The Soviet Union and the communist ideology were in 1950 the United

States' primary enemies. The Republican-dominated United States Congress argued that

Truman's Democrat-led administration was incompetent against the communist threat.

Specifically, the Congress blamed Truman and his administration for allowing

communists to seize political power in China.[484] Such charges, given the United States'

previous support for China's non-communist faction, were politically damaging to

Truman. Thus, it is reasonable to conclude that Acheson sought to appear tough on

---

[482]Freedman, "Introduction," 2.

[483]Lord Moran (Sir Charles Watson), *Churchill: The Struggle for Survival 1945-60* (London: Sphere, 1968), 446-47.

[484]Truman, *Memoirs by Harry S. Truman, Volume II: Years of Trial and Hope*, 430.

communism, and thereby reduce domestic pressure on Truman's administration, through harsh diplomacy with American allies.

Truman maintained primary responsibility for the actions of his administration as it developed a coalition. He was the United States President. Like military commanders, Truman was responsible for everything, good or bad, that his administration accomplished or failed to achieve. It is likely that the 1950 Congressional election and the 1952 Presidential election affected the Truman administration's efforts to satisfy domestic complaints for its softness against communism.

Importantly, the United States Constitution in 1950 did not impose term limits on the American president. Therefore, Truman could run for office again in 1952 if he wanted. Responding effectively to North Korean aggression could aid Truman's goals for the Democratic Party and for his potential reelection. In his memoirs, Truman claimed that he decided in April 1950 against seeking reelection.[485] He later claimed that he did not want another presidential term because he no longer wanted the responsibility.[486] Nevertheless, his administration's conduct demonstrated clear signs that it wanted the Korean War to affect positively its domestic standing.

Efforts by George W. Bush's administration to develop a coalition for Operation Iraqi Freedom (OIF) are comparable to the Truman administration's similar efforts for Korea. Bush's administration developed a coalition to invade Iraq with a "with us or

---

[485]Ibid., 488.

[486]Margaret Truman, ed. *Where the Buck Stops: The Personal and Private Writings of Harry S. Truman* (New York: Warner Books, 1989), 111.

against us"[487] outlook. Terrorist attacks on September 11, 2001 framed the Bush administration's pre-OIF mentality. Bush likely felt that toppling Saddam Hussein's regime supported international security. However, it is also logical to conclude that several of the nations from which Bush's administration pursued military contributions viewed its efforts as motivated to support purely American interests.

The Bush administration's "with or against" approach created diplomatic tactics that a majority of the international community considered uncivil. Bush's administration alienated nations that may have supported an invasion of Iraq with military forces under different circumstances. Importantly, Bush's administration pursued a coalition from a position of influence dissimilar to the Truman administration. America's global leadership position constitutes the primary difference between the Truman and Bush administrations regarding coalition development. Specifically, nations did not rely on American support in 2003 in a manner similar to 1950. This fact is critical as a lesson for current and future American leaders.

The United States does not possess undisputed leadership against an identifiable enemy, such as the Soviet Union, in present times. Furthermore, the United States does not have the loyalty of many nations that rely on American assistance to deter that enemy as it did in 1950. Terrorism is an international threat. However, it does not affect equally every nation. Therefore, future United States government efforts to benefit American or international interests through military operations will have to show more respect than Acheson did to potential nations to receive their contributions of military forces.

---

[487]George W. Bush, "Address to a Joint Session of Congress and the American People, November 6, 2001," http://georgewbush-whitehouse.archives.gov/news/releases/2001/09/20010920-8.html (accessed November 6, 2013).

Two examples reflect an American lack of patience with its Commonwealth partners in Korea. British and Canadian naval support for operations in Korea constitutes the first example. The reception of Canadian land forces to Korea constitutes the second example. In these examples, American political and military leaders forgot that contributions in any form are better than no contributions.

Ten British and three Canadian naval vessels were operating under the UN Command by September 1, 1950.[488] British and Canadian vessels also participated in the Inchon landings.[489] Additional Commonwealth naval support was forthcoming. Regardless, Truman's administration continued to insist that its coalition partners contribute land forces.

Truman's administration was not wrong to pursue land force contributions. The UN Command "urgently needed" land forces during August-September 1950 if it expected to preserve South Korea's sovereignty.[490] The UN Command could not rely on only American and South Korean land forces. Regardless, the Truman administration's lack of patience created adverse effects for Commonwealth soldiers and for the coalition's unity.

---

[488]Status of United Nations Military Assistance Offers, September 1, 1950, 1.

[489]Blaxland, "The Korean War: Reflections on Shared Australian and Canadian Military Experiences," 28.

[490]Report of the United Nations Command Operations in Korea for the period 16-31 August 1950, transmitted by Ambassador Warren R. Austin, U.S. Representative to the United Nations, to the President of the Security Council, September 18, 1950, 8.

Joint Publication 3-16 identifies "even-handed patience" as important for alliances but "equally necessary" regarding prospective coalition partners.[491] According to JP 3-16, coalition partners should receive appreciation for their contributions regardless of type or size. Therefore, British and Canadian naval support should have received some appreciation from Truman's administration. American gratitude should have been abundant given the Commonwealth's, specifically Canada's, inability to provide immediate ground forces. As stated, Truman's administration was under considerable domestic pressure to respond effectively to North Korea's invasion. However, impatience prevented Truman's administration from commending its partners for their contributions.

Coalition leaders must remain patient with a potential contributing nation's limitations, even if those limitations appear disingenuous. Franks and Pearson claimed that global commitments or other considerations limited their ability to contribute land forces. Thus, it is reasonable to conclude that British and Canadian contributions in September 1950 were all those nations could provide at that time. Truman's administration forgot that Commonwealth naval contributions reduced the United States' responsibility to allocate additional American naval power to the Korean War. Furthermore, General Omar Bradley, Chairman of the United States Joint Chiefs of Staff, fretted over the effects of the Korean War on his military's ability to defend the continental United States.[492] Therefore, the Commonwealth's naval contributions enabled

---

[491]Chairman, Joint Chiefs of Staff, Joint Publication 3-16 (2007), x.

[492]U.S. Department of State, Foreign Policy Studies Branch, Chronology of Principle Events Relating to the Korean Conflict, November 1950, 21.

Truman's administration to fulfill other American obligations, to include homeland security. However, Truman's administration appeared to ignore this reality.

The Truman administration's negligence was problematic. It is rational to believe that the United States will provide a preponderance of personnel and materiél to future coalition operations. However, aside from legitimizing an operation with multinational participation, the United States military simply cannot accomplish independently every task involved with coalition operations. Non-American soldiers, for example, eventually provided security at base camps that housed American troops during OIF and Operation Enduring Freedom. These foreign soldiers guarded base entry points and operated perimeter security points.

Foreign soldier contributions enabled American military personnel to focus on their tactical missions in OIF and Operation Enduring Freedom. This statement does not suggest that American soldiers should avoid tasks such as securing base entry control points. Furthermore, this statement does not recommend that foreign soldiers only perform tasks that do not include operations on the battlefield. However, it is likely that valid restrictions limited the size of non-American forces contributed to OIF and Operation Enduring Freedom. Therefore, by applying patience and recognizing that the United States is not acting alone, American soldiers should appreciate foreign soldier participation in future operations regardless of size or type. Appreciation in this form would have simplified the reception of Canadian land forces in Korea.

Lieutenant-Colonel J.R. Stone commanded the first organization of Canadian land forces to arrive in Korea. The 2 PPCLI departed for Korea on the same day that Chinese forces invaded the peninsula.[493] Lieutenant General Walton Walker, the EUSA

commander, wanted to position 2 PPCLI at a forward location immediately after its

arrival. However, St Laurent's government ordered Stone to conduct an eight-week

training period and avoid combat except in cases of self-defense after his battalion

arrived in Korea. Furthermore, the Canadian government allowed Stone to determine

when 2 PPCLI was "fit for operations."[494] Different perspectives created a conflict. Stone

had to produce his government's orders to prevent Walker from committing Canada's

unprepared forces to battle.

From a JP 3-16 perspective, the conflict between Stone and Walker was

avoidable. Walker needed patience for Stone's predicament. Walker's position was

justifiable in one regard. He needed to employ all available land forces to thwart the

Chinese advance. However, Walker did not care to remember, did not know, or forgot

that nations that contribute military forces to a coalition are likely to apply specific

restrictions to the employment of their forces. Such restrictions typically include the

conditions under which their forces operate. For example, a national government may not

want its forces to operate in periods of darkness. Additionally, national governments may

want their forces to conduct only tasks that are unrelated to direct combat.

Joint Publication 3-16 specifically identifies the fact that military commanders

will prioritize their national government's policies over the coalition commander's

directives. National constitutions obligate commanders to do so. An American

---

[493]Johnston, *A War of Patrols: Canadian Army Operations in Korea*, 55.

[494]Stairs, *The Diplomacy of Constraint: Canada, the Korean War, and the United States*, 206.

commander, for example, will always command American forces because the United States Constitution identifies the American President as the Commander-in-Chief of the United States military. Foreign military officers, thus, cannot legally command all American military personnel in a combat environment. This example demonstrates restrictions on the employment of American military forces. Therefore, it is only logical to assume that foreign nations will restrict the employment of their military forces in a coalition.

A nation's reasons for restricting its military forces are legal and non-negotiable. Nations provide forces to a coalition for specific reasons. Therefore, it is only natural that contributing nations will restrict the employment of their military forces to support those aims. Woodrow Wilson, for example did not want American forces to fight under British or French commanders during the First World War. Constitutionality aside, Wilson applied this restriction to the American Expeditionary Forces to ensure his place at the post-war peace conference.[495] National restrictions to the employment of military forces do not require official explanation. Rather, the coalition commander and their subordinates should be thankful for the fact that such military forces are available at all.

Stone's position, thus, was justified. His impulse to utilize his government's orders to justify his arguments with Walker depicted a total lack of American patience at the military level. Walker's behavior reflected Acheson's initial diplomacy. Prussian military theorist Carl von Clausewitz's identification of war as "a continuation of political activity by other means,"[496] therefore, applies to an American commander's

---

[495]Yockelson, *Borrowed Soldiers: Americans under British Command, 1918*, xi.

[496]von Clausewitz, *On War*, 87.

interactions with their coalition partners as much as it does to their enemy. Specifically, Walker's military negotiations with Stone affected American diplomacy with the Canadian government.

The employment of Canadian forces was a concern that required involvement from Canada's national government. For that reason, it is critical for a coalition's military commander to understand their limitations regarding the employment of foreign soldiers. Coalition commanders cannot expect to give orders to foreign forces with the same authority they retain over soldiers from their respective nation. Commanders must remain patient with their coalition partners and utilize their partners' available capabilities to accomplish the mission. Failing to do so is likely to force the national government that contributed such soldiers to reconsider its assistance. Therefore, JP 3-16 correctly identifies patience as important to coalition relationships. A greater American knowledge of its Commonwealth partners and their limitations likely could have prevented the Truman administration's general impatience and events such as the Walker-Stone interactions from affecting coalition unity during the Korean War.

Great Britain's ability to provide land forces to Korea with the speed at which Acheson demanded was clearly limited. Great Britain was involved in a "minor war" in Malaya in June 1950.[497] At the same time, Clement Attlee's government assigned Britain's military forces to Hong Kong, the Middle East, Austria, Trieste, and Germany.[498] Economically, British citizens were still recovering from the Second World

---

[497]Sir Gladwyn Jebb, "The Free World and the United Nations," *Foreign Affairs* 31, no. 3 (April 1953): 389.

[498]Anthony Eden, "Britain in World Strategy," *Foreign Affairs* 29, no. 3 (April 1951): 342.

War. Britain's political leaders understood the financial burdens of a new war in Korea

on their citizens. Therefore, Attlee's government could not merely tell British citizens to

expect "no easement whatsoever" on their economic condition for the near future.[499]

Truman's administration did not understand Britain's limitations.

Truman's administration also did not understand Canada's constraints. 42,000

Canadian soldiers served on active duty in June 1950.[500] However, St Laurent's

government had yet to station troops in Europe as part of the NATO by 1950.[501]

Therefore, it had yet to meet an alliance-based obligation. It is illogical to assume that St

Laurent's government was capable of providing forces to an "*ad hoc* organization"[502]

such as the coalition in Korea. Consequently, the Truman administration's beliefs in

Canada's ability to contribute to a temporary organization were misguided. Knowledge of

partners could have moderated the Truman administration's thought process and actions

vis-à-vis Britain and Canada.

Global commitments and legislative restrictions limited Australia's ability to

commit immediately its land forces. In 1950, Australia's Robert Menzies government

assumed that any war requiring Australian military forces would occur in the Middle East

under the umbrella of the British Commonwealth.[503] Constitutionally, Menzies could not

---

[499]Roy Harrod, "Hands and Fists Across the Sea," *Foreign Affairs* 30, no. 1 (October 1951): 68.

[500]Eayrs, *In Defence of Canada: Growing Up Allied*, 62.

[501]Grey, *The Commonwealth Armies and the Korean War*, 31.

[502]Chairman, Joint Chiefs of Staff, Joint Publication 3-16 (2007), I-1.

[503]Grey, "The Formation of the Commonwealth Division, 1950-51," 12.

force military personnel to serve outside of Australia.[504] Therefore, Menzies' government needed a substantial number of volunteers for operations in Korea to increase the size of its 14,651-person army.[505] Truman's administration appeared to acknowledge Australia's limitations, and interacted with Australian representatives from this position of understanding. Acheson, for example, offered Menzies an aid package to develop Australia's infrastructure without a formal Australian request for such an offer.[506] It is possible that Menzies' government received less "forceful" language than its Commonwealth counterparts did because Truman's administration identified greater commonality with Australia and its government. Regardless, JP 3-16 reflects the positive experience of American-Australian diplomacy after June 25, 1950.

The purpose of discussing American impatience with British Commonwealth governments in 1950 is to identify the fact that military assistance can appear from unexpected sources. Australia was not a United States ally in June 1950. However, Australian troops were among the best forces within the UN Command. El Salvador and the Republic of Georgia, among other nations, were not necessarily American allies in 2003. However, they committed troops to the American-led coalition for OIF.[507] El

---

[504]O'Neill, *Australia in the Korean War 1950-53. Volume I: Strategy and Diplomacy*, 33.

[505]Blaxland, "The Korean War: Reflections on Shared Australian and Canadian Military Experiences," 27.

[506]Memorandum of Conversation: Korea; Migration Program; Requirement for Funds, between Dean Acheson and Robert Menzies, July 31, 1950, Papers of Dean Acheson, Harry S. Truman Library, Independence, MO.

[507]Stephan A. Carney, CMH Pub 59-3-1, *Allied Participation in Operation Iraqi Freedom* (Washington, DC: Center of Military History), 3. http://www.history.army.mil/html/books/059/59-3-1/CMH_59-3-1.pdf (accessed November 7, 2013).

Salvadorian and Georgian contributions to OIF demonstrated that military support for coalitions is available from unexpected sources.

The United States government likely did not expect El Salvador or Georgia to contribute anything to OIF. El Salvador limited its troops to civil-military operations.[508] Among other tasks, Georgian forces provided security to the UN compound in Iraq.[509] El Salvadorian and Georgian contributions did not affect significantly operations in Iraq. However, they reduced American responsibilities to perform those missions.

Governments that seek to build a coalition must demonstrate sufficient knowledge of potential partners to gain such contributions. Coalition developers must first understand that unrequested assistance will not produce contributions. Second, coalition developers must acknowledge the limitations of the nations from which they seek support and show thanks for any contributions those nations make. Third, coalition developers, and the forces they contribute, should be grateful for such contributions regardless of the motive behind them. Finally, coalition developers should recognize that there are times when potential coalition partners, such as Canada in 1950, simply cannot contribute materially to military operations. Therefore, JP 3-16 correctly recommends that coalition leaders understand their partners' limitations and capabilities as they develop and sustain a coalition.

Joint Publication 3-16 identifies political goals as the decisive factor of a nation's decision to contribute or refrain from contributing forces to a coalition. Thailand, Bolivia, and Turkey announced their intentions by July 26, 1950 to send ground forces to

---

[508]Ibid., 4.

[509]Ibid., 63.

Korea.[510] Menzies' government announced that Australia would provide military forces to Korea one hour prior to the Attlee government's announcement.[511] Menzies' timing prompted Attlee's government to deploy immediately forces from its garrison in Hong Kong to Korea.[512] St Laurent's government passed legislation to increase the size of its army.[513] Additionally, it deployed an unprepared battalion to Korea and suspended participation in a European naval exercise so that it could send immediately naval forces to Korea.[514]

The examples mentioned specifically demonstrate JP 3-16's identification of the primacy nations affix to political goals and interests when committing military forces to a coalition. Thai, Bolivian, and Turkish announcements followed immediately Truman's announcement that he planned to send American forces to Korea. Therefore, Thailand, Bolivia, and Turkey demonstrated their solidarity with Truman's administration. The timing of Australia's announcement created a perception that it was a more reliable American partner than Great Britain. Attlee attempted to negate this perception by rushing forces to Korea. St Laurent understood that his nation needed to contribute forces in some form to maintain Canada's national prestige, credibility, and influence with the United States and the UN.

---

[510]U.S. Department of State, World Reaction to Korean Developments, No. 27, July 24, 1950; No. 29, July 26, 1950.

[511]Grey, *The Commonwealth Armies and the Korean War*, 35.

[512]Ibid., 57.

[513]Eayrs, *In Defence of Canada: Growing Up Allied*, 62.

[514]U.S. Department of State, *U.S. Policy in the Korean Crisis*, 33.

National objectives clearly inspired each nation's decision to participate in the Korean War. However, Canadian and Australian governments had additional reason to provide forces. Specifically, they understood that they could no longer rely on Britain for their national security. World War II changed the foundation of the British Commonwealth. Great Britain was not in 1950 the dominant political, military, and economic power that it was prior to 1945. Therefore, its "obstreperous children"[515] understood in 1950 that the United States alone was capable of securing their interests. Supporting the United States in Korea was a critical means for these nations to ensure American assistance for their national security interests. Security concerns, therefore, prompted Australian and Canadian representatives to withstand the worst of the Truman administration's tactics.

The United States and Canada share a long border. Potential Soviet attacks against the continental United States threatened Canadian security. Therefore, it is reasonable to conclude that Louis St Laurent contributed Canadian forces to Korea to ensure American protection for his country if such an event occurred. Robert Menzies contributed Australian forces to Korea because his government wanted a Pacific-region security agreement with the United States. Specifically, Menzies' government believed that American military strength could guarantee Australian security by negating a "possible resurgence of Japanese or Communist militarism"[516] in the Pacific and thereby guarantee Australia's security.

---

[515]U.S. Department of State, *Foreign Relations of the United States, 1948,* vol. 6, 753.

[516]Robert Gordon Menzies, "The Pacific Settlement Seen from Australia," *Foreign Affairs* 31, no. 2 (January 1952): 195.

Gavan McCormack argued that Australia's contributions to Korea were a Menzies government attempt to "cash in on American good will."[517] Regardless of McCormack's intent, his argument clearly identified that political goals, and Commonwealth reliance on American protection, motivated Canadian and Australian decision to contribute forces to the Korean War. Thus, JP 3-16 correctly identified the heavy influence that political objectives have on a nation's decision to contribute to a coalition. United States political and military leaders would be remiss to ignore this reality.

Nations contribute forces to coalitions with the expectation that they will gain a political advantage. They do not necessarily contribute forces to coalitions for purely moral purposes. The Republic of Georgia, for example, contributed forces to OIF to enhance its prospects for membership in NATO.[518] Therefore, United States leaders should not consider multinational contribution offers as a sign of benevolence. Additionally, United States political and military leaders have another reason for caution. Specifically, JP 3-16 advises American leaders to avoid expectations of automatic contributions from nations that are American allies. Its admonition in this case applies to American political leaders as well as military personnel. Truman's administration likely created the reason for the inclusion of this guidance in JP 3-16.

---

[517]Colin Mackerras, review of *Cold War, Hot War, An Australian Perspective on the Korean War*, by Gavan McCormack, *The Australian Journal of Chinese Affairs* no. 11 (January 1984): 189.

[518]Jim Nichol, *Georgia [Republic]: Recent Developments and U.S. Interests* (Washington, DC: Congressional Research Service, 2012), 4.

Dean Acheson threatened his Commonwealth allies with "a wave of isolationism in the United States"[519] to gain their contributions for Korea. Specifically, his warnings proposed to withhold American military and financial support for his Commonwealth allies if they did not assist the United States in Korea. Therefore, Acheson's demands of Sir Oliver Franks and Lester Pearson revealed his expectations for automatic contributions from American allies. Acheson should have avoided these expectations.

Clement Attlee's government, for example, assigned its military forces to numerous locations throughout the world. British military commitments in 1950 included a contribution of forces to NATO. Acheson's expectations of an ally ignored that ally's contributions to the cause for which the alliance was established. This thesis previously discussed Canada's inability to contribute to NATO. However, Attlee had to remove British troops from Hong Kong, a critical British possession, to provide an immediate British presence in Korea. Therefore, it is entirely logical to conclude that Great Britain, in addition to Canada, did not have available the land forces demanded by Truman's administration. Attlee's desire to prove his nation's credibility as a reliable American partner was impressive given Britain's military and economic limitations.

Truman's administration clearly did not understand, or otherwise ignored, British and Canadian limitations. American expectations for automatic contributions from allies were problematic for coalition and NATO unity. George W. Bush's administration repeated Acheson's tactics while pursuing French military assistance for Operation Iraqi Freedom. France was an American ally in NATO. Economic and military limitations did

---

[519]Dockrill, "The Foreign Office, Anglo-American Relations and the Korean War, June 1950-June 1951," 468.

198

not affect France's ability to contribute forces to support OIF. However, it did not share American political goals for Iraq. France, thus, did not contribute military forces to OIF.

American proposals to rename French Fries as "Freedom Fries" in 2003 demonstrated the reduction of popular unity between the United States and France. The Bush administration's expectations of automatic support from an ally for a coalition operation provoked this reduction. Therefore, it is critical for American political and military leaders to remember that allies do not always share mutual goals with the United States. JP 3-16's discussion of this fact gains more importance when coalition commanders employ foreign military forces.

Aside from Walton Walker's initial interactions with Canadian forces, one critical example from the Korean War demonstrated a coalition commander's limitations regarding the employment of foreign forces. Initially, only American personnel provided security at Koje-Do. Koje-Do was a prisoner of war camp. Subsequently General Mark Clarke assigned non-American forces, including Canadian personnel, to conduct security operations at Koje-Do. Clarke assigned multinational forces to Koje-Do to reduce international pressure on the United States after communist prisoners subjected anti-communist prisoners to beatings and other methods of intimidation.[520] However, Clarke did not consult Canada's St Laurent government prior to assigning Canadian personnel to Koje-Do.[521]

---

[520]Stairs, *The Diplomacy of Constraint: Canada, the Korean War, and the United States*, 246.

[521]Blaxland, "The Korean War: Reflections on Shared Australian and Canadian Military Experiences," 31.

Canada's official historian for the Korean War, Herbert Fairlie Wood, admitted that St Laurent's government "made too much fuss over the affair."[522] Wood's admission is irrelevant. His admission occurred more than a decade after the Korean War ended. Admissions after the fact, such as Wood's, do not change the fact that Canadian stubbornness damaged relations with the Truman administration. However, Wood's admission demonstrated three of JP 3-16's relevant ideas.

First, foreign nations are likely to restrict the forces they provide for coalitions to specific operations. Such restrictions support national goals. Second, contributing nations validly expect to remain informed regarding the employment of their forces in a coalition structure. The United States government, for example, has to satisfy its domestic audience. Western nations share the same responsibility. Third, coalition commanders must understand their partners' goals. Understanding a partner's goals supports a coalition commander's acknowledgement and application of the first two points.

Military necessity may require a commander to utilize foreign forces in conditions for which they are unprepared. Clarke, as the coalition commander, was not legally required to inform St Laurent's government of his decision. However, St Laurent's government deserved inclusion in the decision-making process that prompted Clark to assign Canadian forces to Koje-Do. Furthermore, employment of this nature should remain an option of last resort. Future American commanders would be wise to heed such lessons. Identifying strategic goals is a method to avoid situations that employ foreign forces in operations unsanctioned by their respective governments.

---

[522]Wood, *Strange Battleground: Official History of the Canadian Army in Korea*, 196.

Joint Publication 3-16 accurately identifies strategic objectives as a cornerstone of coalition development.[523] Strategic objectives define the goals that a political leader wants to achieve through military operations. Additionally, it sustains a coalition until its mission is complete. Therefore, positive coalition relationships rely as heavily on the strategic objective as they do on operational successes or failures.

According to JP 3-16, the importance of the strategic objective demands that coalition developers determine the strategic objective prior to committing military forces. Moreover, coalition developers should establish the strategic objective as a means to help nations determine if they will contribute forces to the coalition. Two Korean War examples demonstrated the effects of identifying strategic objectives on efforts to build and sustain coalitions. Harry Truman's initial guidance for operations in Korea, provided in July 1950, constitutes the first example. Second, Truman decided to cross the 38th Parallel in October 1950.

Truman's initial guidance for operations in Korea was critical to coalition development. He identified the conflict as a "police action"[524] to limit the conflict. Furthermore, he directed his military commanders to achieve only the UN mandate of defending South Korea's sovereignty. Additionally, Truman wanted to keep the war localized to Korea to avoid an escalation of the war through Chinese or Soviet participation. Truman applied specific restrictions to his military commanders to ensure that they did not violate his guidance while accomplishing the UN objective.

---

[523]Chairman, Joint Chiefs of Staff, Joint Publication 3-16 (2007), III-3.

[524]U.S. Department of State, White House Press and Radio News Conference, President Harry S. Truman, June 29, 1950.

Potential coalition partners, such as the Commonwealth governments, feared an escalation of the war. Truman's regulations created conditions that were favorable for potential coalition partners to provide military forces. Truman's restrictions, such as denying his military commanders' requests to conduct aerial reconnaissance near Korea's borders with the Soviet Union and China,[525] prevented the likelihood of war in Korea with the communist nations. Truman, in this example, demonstrated knowledge of his partners and engendered their contributions. Unfortunately, Truman's decision to cross the 38th Parallel reversed his initial success.

All American and British political parties appeared to support crossing the 38th Parallel.[526] However, non-partisan support for this matter was irrelevant. Political leaders allowed military success to influence their decision-making. Therefore, crossing the 38th Parallel to unify Korea was a critical mistake. It prompted China to invade Korea. More importantly, however, crossing the 38th Parallel created conditions that diminished the political and military unity between Truman's administration and its Commonwealth coalition partners.

American and Commonwealth perceptions of the "uselessness"[527] of the Korean War did not begin until after the Chinese invaded Korea. American citizens lost

---

[525]U.S. Department of State, Memorandum of Conversation, Dean Rusk, Assistant Secretary of State and Brigadier General P. Hamilton, U.S. Air Force, July 6, 1950, Harry S. Truman Library, Independence, MO.

[526]Peter Lowe, "An Ally and a Recalcitrant General: Great Britain, Douglas MacArthur and the Korean War, 1950-51," *The English Historical Review* 105, no. 416 (July 1990): 652.

[527]Adlai Stevenson, "Korea in Perspective," *Foreign Affairs* 30, no. 3 (April 1952): 354.

confidence in the Truman administration's leadership in Korea and, thus, in the coalition, once the war appeared unwinnable.[528] Changing the strategic objective and crossing the 38th Parallel prompted these events. Therefore, future coalition developers would be wise to heed the lessons of the Truman administration's decision to change its strategic objective for Korea.

President George H.W. Bush appeared to learn from Truman's mistakes when he sent American military forces to Saudi Arabia in 1990. Bush, through UN approval, built a coalition to defend Saudi Arabia and expel the Iraqi Army from Kuwait. Bush correctly decided to halt the coalition's advance after it accomplished its mission. He did not let military success, achieved in a period of 100 hours, dictate the coalition's political objective. Coalition members contributed forces to expel Iraq from Kuwait. They did not contribute military forces to topple the Iraqi government. Therefore, the coalition's unity would have crumbled had Bush decided to conquer Iraq. Bush's thoughtfulness and thoroughness demonstrated characteristics from which future coalition leaders would be wise to learn and replicate.

Five lessons from the Truman administration's leadership in Korea do not appear in JP 3-16. First, Truman's administration developed a coalition to defend another country. Second, a subordinate coalition partner proposed to change the coalition's objective. Third, poor performance by some American units in Korea reduced Commonwealth opinions of the United States' credibility. Fourth, American representatives negotiated an armistice with the Chinese without a real understanding of

_____

[528]Dingman, "Atomic Diplomacy during the Korean War," 70.

203

Chinese culture. Finally, American commanders appeared to disregard the negative effects of heavy casualties on Commonwealth support for the Korean War.

Rhee Syngman was the Truman administration's most important ally during the Korean War. Rhee did not gain this status through his nation's military contributions to the Korean War. He was the Republic of Korea's President. His earned his position through a democratic election that validated by the UN. Therefore, Truman's decisions had to consider Rhee's objectives as much, if not more, than Commonwealth objectives.

Rhee would not accept anything less than a united Korea under his authority until President Dwight D. Eisenhower convinced him in 1953 to pursue Korean unification through non-military means.[529] It is logical to conclude that Rhee influenced significantly Truman's decision to cross the 38th Parallel. Additionally, the armistice for Korea required Rhee's approval. His boycott of the negotiations in May 1953 prolonged their conduct, thereby extending the war and creating more casualties on both sides.[530] Regardless, Rhee's position as South Korea's president justified his goals and influence.

Hamid Karzai, the President of Afghanistan, replicated Rhee's actions more than fifty years after the Korean War. Karzai, for example, refused to negotiate with the Taliban to end the war in his country. His refusal prolonged American efforts to end the war in Afghanistan. Additionally, Rhee and Karzai depended heavily on American economic and military assistance to sustain their governments. Therefore, Rhee's effects on the Korean War are important to the present and future.

---

[529]Truman, *Memoirs by Harry S. Truman. Volume Two: Years of Trial and Hope*, 462.

[530]Acheson, *The Korean War*, 150.

Rhee and Karzai's reliance on American support does not mean that they would, or should, bow meekly to American whims. Any criticism of Karzai's public disapproval for American policies ignores his legal status as the sovereign leader of Afghanistan. Politically, neither Truman's administration nor the George W. Bush or Barack Obama administrations could afford to abandon their respective allies. To do so would reduce United States credibility in the world. JP 3-16 pays no attention to these facts.

Joint Publication 3-16 also does not discuss the possibility that a coalition member may recommend changes to the strategic objective. Clement Attlee's government made such a recommendation. It proposed a resolution that would pursue a "unified, independent and democratic" Korean government.[531] The UN approved this resolution on October 7, 1950. The resolution extended the war in time for the UN Command. Specifically, the war could have ended in October 1950 after all North Korean forces were expelled from South Korea.

Concerns of this nature should not affect coalition operations. Nations should understand and accept a coalition's strategic objective prior to contributing forces. Britain's proposal, apparently suggested without consultation with Truman's administration, created conditions that led to the Chinese invasion in Korea. China's involvement prolonged the war and created more casualties. Unfortunately, the UN Command was close to achieving its original objective when Britain proposed to unify Korea.

---

[531]Fitzsimmons, *The Foreign Policy of the British Labour Government 1945-1951*, 136.

Extending the war in October 1950 threatened the UN Command's ability to negotiate from a position of strength. JP 3-16 stresses the importance of the strategic objective to developing and sustaining a coalition. The publication should also stress the objective's permanence as a means to sustain a coalition. Otherwise, circumstances that arose in Korea are likely to arise in future coalition operations.

Poor American combat performance after the initial Chinese invasion was one such circumstance of the war's extension. The United States was clearly the lead nation in Korea. JP 3-16 defines a coalition's "lead nation" as the nation with sufficient "will and capability, competence, and influence" to lead coalition operations.[532] It mentions the terms "competence" and "performance" sparingly. It briefly discusses the coalition commander's responsibility to determine a military organization's "training-level competence" before committing that force to combat.[533] JP 3-16 uses the term "performance" only to mention that military forces are likely to receive orders directing them to conduct tasks, such as advising government officials, which ordinarily are civilian tasks.

The EUSA defeated North Korean forces in South Korea. However, the Chinese invasion caused EUSA to retreat hastily "in jeeps and trucks from an overwhelming horde . . . following on mules, ponies, and camels.[534] British and Australian confidence in American land forces "declined considerably" after observing EUSA's retreat.[535] Poor

---

[532]Chairman, Joint Chiefs of Staff, Joint Publication 3-16 (2013), C-3.

[533]Chairman, Joint Chiefs of Staff, Joint Publication 3-16 (2007), III-5.

[534]Gallaway, *The Last Call of the Bugle: The Long Road to Kapyong*, 170.

[535]Grey, "The Regiment's First War: Korea, 1950-56," 66.

206

Commonwealth opinions of American combat capabilities reduced the United States' credibility and, thus, the Truman administration's ability to lead effectively the coalition in Korea.

Joint Publication 3-16 neglects to advise the United States military that its actions in combat reflect American political will, capability, competence, influence, credibility, and, therefore the United States' ability to lead a coalition. This omission is problematic because it is critical for American military personnel to remember continuously that they represent America's government and citizens in peace and war. They must also remember that their actions when interacting with foreigners also affect foreign perceptions of the United States.

American military personnel deployed to Operations Enduring and Iraqi Freedom received substantial briefings on the cultures with which they would interact. Presenters continually emphasized the importance of respecting those cultures. However, JP 3-16 fails to review respect for the enemy's culture. Its oversight is glaring. It is also problematic because future coalition operations are unlikely to replicate the conditions in Iraq or Afghanistan. Specifically, except for the initial invasion of Iraq in 2003, coalitions that deployed to those nations did not make war against an enemy government. Rather, coalitions conducted operations in Iraq and Afghanistan to support and develop new governments. However, making war against an enemy government is not necessarily outdated as a form of warfare.

Government against government warfare occurred in Korea. It can occur again. Americans negotiators ignored Chinese culture in their pursuit of an armistice to end the Korean War. Indirect Chinese language and negotiating feints and ploys frustrated the

American negotiators' preference for direct language. Furthermore, American negotiators forgot that China's government, like Truman's administration, wanted to attain goals that benefitted its interests. Unfortunately, American ignorance of Chinese culture contributed to protracted negotiations and, thus, more casualties in Korea.

Joint Publication 3-16 advises American military personnel to show respect and patience for multinational contributions in detail. Additionally, JP 3-16 cautions its readers to remain respectful and patient toward the reason why multinational forces are committed and the justification behind any restrictions under which they operate. Critically, American military personnel demonstrate these traits by developing their knowledge of their partners. However, JP 3-16 needs to discuss respect for the enemy's culture and perspectives at the highest levels of the United States government and military. Furthermore, American leaders need to understand, as Truman's administration failed to, that impatience with enemy negotiators adversely affects battlefield operations. Such impatience creates negative effects on domestic morale within the coalition's contributing nations.

The Commonwealth nations could not afford substantial casualties for political and military reasons.[536] Politically, nations such as Great Britain were still recovering from World War II in 1950. Additionally, the Korean War threatened directly neither British nor Canadian vital interests. Therefore, the Attlee and St Laurent governments would find themselves hard-pressed to justify heavy casualties to their constituents in a conflict that did not threaten their national livelihoods. The United States military seeks

---

[536]Blaxland, "The Korean War: Reflections on Shared Australian and Canadian Military Experiences," 30.

to minimize its casualties when conducting military operations. It does this to retain public support for its efforts. Thus, American leaders should instantaneously assume that coalition partners share the same perspective.

Militarily, Commonwealth units in Korea were smaller than were their American counterparts.[537] Commonwealth formations were not suited for the "meat grinder"[538] tactics that General Matthew Ridgway adopted after the war grew into a stalemate. Furthermore, Chinese and North Korean forces were "of approximately equal strength and determination" to the UN Command.[539] Therefore, battles incurring equal casualties on both sides put the Commonwealth forces at a disadvantage. These concerns became problematic after the Korean War stalemated and representatives negotiated armistice terms.

Effective coalitions rely on the morale and willpower of all contributing nations. American generals commanded the International Security Assistance Force (ISAF) in support of Operation Enduring Freedom. The International Security Assistance Force commander also served as the commander of all American forces. Therefore, future coalition commanders cannot concern themselves with only their respective nation's morale or willpower. They command entire coalition and, thus, must include multinational considerations and perspectives in their decision-making. Unfortunately,

---

[537]Ibid.

[538]Herring, *From Colony to Superpower: U.S. Foreign Relations since 1776*, 644.

[539]Weigley, *The American Way of War: A History of United States Military Strategy and Policy*, 393.

JP 3-16 does not discuss the negative effects that heavy casualties in the course of coalition operations have on a nation's morale and, thus, coalition unity.

American military leaders published JP 3-16 for American military personnel. United States military leaders are unlikely to demand that their civilian leaders read and apply JP 3-16. To do so would likely create a perception that military personnel are attempting to enforce their will on their civilian leaders. However, JP 3-16's tenets, principles, and guidance apply to American political leaders as much as they do to members of the United States military. Truman's administration provided sufficient evidence to confirm the relationship between JP 3-16's content and American political leaders.

Joint Publication 3-16 promotes coalition unity as something gained through patience, knowledge of partners, and "genuine respect."[540] It is inconceivable to believe that tenets describing the ethics of basic human interaction apply to military but not political personnel. Furthermore, it is highly probable that military leaders will follow their political leaders' example in their treatment of coalition partners. Dean Acheson, for example, utilized a percentage-based system to determine the significance of his coalition partners' contribution levels.[541]

The Truman administration's approach to coalition development was not patient. It certainly was not respectful. Specifically, its poor knowledge, or ignorance, of its partners' limitations provoked its behavior. American military personnel were likely to

---

[540]Chairman, Joint Chiefs of Staff, Joint Publication 3-16 (2007), I-3.

[541]Memorandum of Conversation: Proposed UK Note Relating to Increased Military Effort; China, Dean Acheson and Sir Oliver Franks, August 3, 1950, 1. Papers of Dean Acheson, Harry S. Truman Library, Independence, MO.

replicate the administration's behavior with their Commonwealth counterparts. Lieutenant General Walton Walker's initial interactions with Canada's Lieutenant-Colonel J.R. Stone, for example, demonstrates that Walker imitated Acheson's behavior.

Military coalitions are comparable to the institution of marriage. Human thoughts, emotions, limitations, capabilities, and character influence the conduct of either organization. The only difference between the two is that partners expect marriage to last forever. In contrast, coalitions last only until they achieve their political objective. Regardless, partners hope to gain something by entering a coalition or marriage. Such goals vary by individual. Goals upon entering a marriage include, among others, considerations such as creating a family or improving one's financial status. Goals upon contributing military forces to a coalition include, among others, economic assistance, military aid, or a greater diplomatic position in the world.

Arguments that utilize the size of a nation's military contribution, such as Acheson's percentage-based approach, or the wealth an individual brings to a marriage to define significance are irrelevant. Such arguments are harmful to a marriage or coalition's unity and success. Truman, Attlee, St Laurent, and Menzies united their nations to achieve a common purpose. Different goals motivated each man to include his nation in the Korean War. Additionally, different objectives inspired the public and private comments, thoughts, and behaviors of each man, and their respective governments, until an armistice ended the cause for which they created their coalition.

Unfortunately, the Truman administration's interactions with its Commonwealth partners created problems that extended beyond the Korean War. Truman's administration and Britain's Clement Attlee government, for example, "bequeathed" their diplomatic problems to their replacements.[542] Dwight D. Eisenhower, Truman's

successor as United States President, believed that Anglo-American relations in 1953

were at their worst point since 1945.[543] In 1918, Canada's government informed Britain's

government that it would not agree to British policies that threatened Canada's

relationship with the United States.[544] However, Dean Acheson and Lester Pearson,

Canada's Minister for External Affairs, disagreed on the size and significance of

Canada's contributions and, thus, the Louis St Laurent government's ability to influence

vital decisions regarding the war.[545] Therefore, the Korean War ended the "easy and

automatic" relations enjoyed between the United States and Canada.[546]

The critical lesson from this example is the effect of personalities on coalition

sustainment. The personalities of Franklin Roosevelt, Winston Churchill, and Dwight D.

Eisenhower, for example, sustained the Anglo-American coalition during the Second

World War. Each man maintained personal and national interests. However, their

personal and national interests frequently differed. Roosevelt's interests, for example, did

not always align with Churchill's goals. Regardless, each man set aside their individual

interests for the benefit of their partnership.

---

[542]Lowe, "An Ally and a Recalcitrant General: Great Britain, Douglas MacArthur and the Korean War, 1950-51," 652.

[543]Lowe, "The Significance of the Korean War in Anglo-American Relations, 1950-53," 145.

[544]Stevenson, "Canada, Free and Dependent," 458.

[545]Lester B. Pearson, "The Development of Canadian Foreign Policy," *Foreign Affairs* 30, no. 1 (October 1951): 29.

[546]Holmes, "Canada and the United States in World Politics," 105.

Different personalities managed Anglo-American relations during the Korean War. American personalities in particular appeared unable to set aside their national interests in a manner similar to Roosevelt, Churchill, and Eisenhower. Unfortunately, such personalities did not appear to consider the long-term effects of their actions. Specifically, Truman's administration demonstrated a willingness to sacrifice long-term diplomatic relations with the British Commonwealth to achieve a short-term objective in Korea. Future American leaders would be wise to replicate George H.W. Bush's example rather than Truman's example if they determine that a coalition operation is necessary to achieve American goals.

American-Australian relations appear as the only American-Commonwealth relationship that improved during the Korean War. For example, the United States government agreed to a Pacific security pact that included Australia and New Zealand in 1952. The ANZUS did not attach the United States to Australian security in a manner similar to Western Europe and the NATO. However, ANZUS allowed Australia conduct diplomacy with the United States on an equal basis while both nations pursued mutual interests in the Pacific. Australia's "early participation" in the Korean War persuaded Truman's administration to agree to ANZUS.[547]

Joint Publication 3-16 does not identify the source of its content. It is possible that recent coalition operations, such as Operations Enduring and Iraqi Freedom, prompted the document's production. However, strong evidence exists to suggest that efforts by Harry S. Truman's administration to develop and sustain a coalition for the Korean War created JP 3-16's content. Truman's administration included nations with which it

---

[547]Millar, "Australia and the American Alliance," 149.

maintained friendly relations prior to 1950 in its coalition. Its coalition development methods, specifically with its allies, were often questionable and, therefore, unsupportive of its coalition development efforts. The Truman administration's methods were often harsh, demanding, and, in some cases, unforgiving. Truman's administration continued these tactics throughout the duration of the Korean War.

Domestic political concerns and the pressure of war in Korea likely prompted the Truman administration's behavior. However, its conduct created negative long-term effects on American diplomacy. This is significant to the United States because its political and military personnel are likely to work with multinational partners to negate international security threats in the future. Therefore, current and future American political and military leaders, and the subordinates that follow them, would be wise to heed the Truman administration's Korean War example and learn from JP 3-16. Replicating the Truman administration's diplomatic examples will only damage United States credibility and diplomatic relations. Furthermore, it will reduce the willingness of foreign nations to contribute forces to future coalition operations that the United States government considers essential to American interests and international security.

BIBLIOGRAPHY

Primary Sources

Books

Acheson, Dean. *The Korean War*. New York: W.W. Norton & Company, 1971.

Churchill, Winston S. *Blood, Sweat, and Tears*. New York: G. P. Putnam's Sons, 1941.

———. *Victory. War Speeches by the Right Hon. Winston S. Churchill*. Compiled by Charles Eade. Boston: Little, Brown and Company, 1946.

Dennet, Raymond, and Robert K. Turner. eds. *Documents on American Foreign Relations, Vol. XII, January 1–December 31, 1950*. Princeton: Princeton University Press, 1951.

Eden, Anthony. *The Reckoning*. Boston: Houghton Mifflin Company, 1965.

Eisenhower, Dwight D. *Crusade in Europe*. New York: Doubleday & Company, 1948.

Ferrell, Robert H. ed. *Off The Record: The Private Papers of Harry S. Truman*. New York: Harper & Row, 1980.

MacArthur, Douglas. *Reminiscences*. New York: Da Capo Press, 1964.

Miller, Merle. *Plain Speaking: An Oral Biography of Harry S. Truman*. New York: G. P. Putnam's Sons, 1974.

Ridgway, Matthew B. *The Korean War*. Garden City, NY: Doubleday & Company, 1967.

Truman, Harry S. *Memoirs by Harry S. Truman, Volume I: Year of Decisions*. Garden City, NY: Doubleday & Company, 1955.

———. *Memoirs by Harry S. Truman, Volume II: Years of Trial and Hope*. Garden City, NY: Doubleday & Company, 1956.

Truman, Margaret. ed. *Where the Buck Stops: The Personal and Private Writings of Harry S. Truman*. New York: Warner Books, 1989.

Periodicals

Eden, Anthony. "Britain in World Strategy." *Foreign Affairs* 29, no. 3 (April 1951): 341-50.

Menzies, Robert Gordon. "The Pacific Settlement Seen from Australia." *Foreign Affairs* 31, no. 2 (January 1952): 188-96.

Pearson, Lester B. "The Development of Canadian Foreign Policy." *Foreign Affairs* 30, no. 1 (October 1951): 17-30.

Government Documents

Chairman, Joint Chiefs of Staff. Joint Publication 3-16, *Multinational Operations*. Washington, DC: Government Printing Office, 2007.

————. Joint Publication 3-16, *Multinational Operations*. Washington, DC: Government Printing Office, 2013.

The President. *National Security Strategy*. Washington, DC: The White House, 2010. http://www.whitehouse.gov/sites/default/files/rss_viewer/national_security_strate gy.pdf (accessed August 14, 2013).

Harry S. Truman Library

Papers of Dean Acheson

Memorandum of Conversation: Aid to Korea, Truman, Menzies, Acheson, July 28, 1950. Papers of Dean Acheson, Harry S. Truman Library, Independence, MO.

Memorandum of Conversation: Cabinet Meeting, July 14, 1950. Papers of Dean Acheson, Harry S. Truman Library, Independence, MO.

Memorandum of Conversation: Formosa; Contribution of Troops by Canada, Dean Acheson and Lester B. Pearson, July 29, 1950. Papers of Dean Acheson, Harry S. Truman Library, Independence, MO.

Memorandum of Conversation: Korea; Migration Program; Requirement for Funds, between Dean Acheson and Robert Menzies, July 31, 1950. Papers of Dean Acheson. Harry S. Truman Library, Independence, MO.

Memorandum of Conversation: Military Support for Southern Korea, June 29, 1950. Papers of Dean Acheson, Harry S. Truman Library, Independence, MO.

Memorandum of Conversation: Notes on National Security Council Meeting, November 28, 1950. Papers of Dean Acheson, Harry S. Truman Library, Independence, MO.

Memorandum of Conversation: Proposed UK Note Relating to Increased Military Effort; China, Dean Acheson and Sir Oliver Franks, August 3, 1950. Papers of Dean Acheson, Harry S. Truman Library, Independence, MO.

Papers of George M. Elsey

Memo from George M. Elsey to the National Security Council, July 12, 1950. Papers of George M. Elsey, Harry S. Truman Library, Independence, MO.

President Truman's Conversation with George M. Elsey, June 26, 1950. Papers of George M. Elsey, Harry S. Truman Library, Independence, MO.

President's Meeting with Congressional Leaders, July 30, 1950. Papers of George M. Elsey, Harry S. Truman Library, Independence, MO.

Statement by the President, July 8, 1950. Papers of George M. Elsey, Harry S. Truman Library, Independence, MO.

United Nations–Major Developments, April-June, July 5, 1950. Papers of George M. Elsey, Harry S. Truman Library, Independence, MO.

Papers of Harry S. Truman

Building the Peace. Foreign Affairs Outlines no. 24, Autumn 1950. Files of Charles Murphy. President's Secretary's Files. Papers of Harry S. Truman, Harry S. Truman Library, Independence, MO.

President's Secretary's Files

Status of United Nations Military Assistance Offers, September 1, 1950. President's Secretary's Files, Harry S. Truman Library, Independence, MO.

Status of United Nations Military Assistance Offers, October 6, 1950. President's Secretary's Files, Harry S. Truman Library, Independence, MO.

Syngman Rhee, letter to Harry S. Truman, July 17, 1950. President's Secretary's Files, Harry S. Truman Library, Independence, MO.

U.S. Department of State

Foreign Policy Studies Branch. Chronology of Principle Events Relating to the Korean Conflict, June-July 1950. Harry S. Truman Library, Independence, MO.

———. Chronology of Principle Events Relating to the Korean Conflict, September 1950. Harry S. Truman Library, Independence, MO.

———. Chronology of Principle Events Relating to the Korean Conflict, October 1950. Harry S. Truman Library, Independence, MO.

———. Chronology of Principle Events Relating to the Korean Conflict, November 1950. Harry S. Truman Library, Independence, MO.

———. Chronology of Principle Events Relating to the Korean Conflict, December 1950. Harry S. Truman Library, Independence, MO.

———. Chronology of Principle Events Relating to the Korean Conflict, January 1951. Harry S. Truman Library, Independence, MO.

———. Chronology of Principle Events Relating to the Korean Conflict, February 1951. Harry S. Truman Library, Independence, MO.

———. Chronology of Principle Events Relating to the Korean Conflict, March 1951. Harry S. Truman Library, Independence, MO.

———. Chronology of Principle Events Relating to the Korean Conflict, April 1951. Harry S. Truman Library, Independence, MO.

U.S. Department of State. *Foreign Relations of the United States, 1947, The British Commonwealth, Europe*. Vol. 3. Washington, DC: Government Printing Office, 1972.

———. *Foreign Affairs of the United States 1948. General, The United Nations*. Vol. 1, Part One. Washington, DC: Government Printing Office, 1975.

———. *Foreign Affairs of the United States, 1948. General, The United Nations*. Vol. 1, Part Two. Washington, DC: United States Government Printing Office, 1976.

———. *Foreign Relations of the United States, 1948. The Far East and Australia*. Vol. 6. Washington, DC: United States Government Printing Office, 1974.

———. *Foreign Relations of the United States 1950. Western Europe*. Vol. 3. Washington, DC: Government Printing Office, 1977.

———. *U.S. Policy in the Korean Crisis*. Washington, DC: Government Printing Office, 1950.

———. Memorandum of Conversation, U.S./U.K. Discussions on Present World Situation, 20-24 July 1950, General Omar Bradley, Ambassador Phillip C. Jessup and Sir Oliver Franks, Lord Tedder. Harry S. Truman Library, Independence, MO.

———. Memorandum of Conversation, General Omar Bradley, Ambassador Phillip C. Jessup, July 12, 1950. Harry S. Truman Library, Independence, MO.

———. Message from Mr. Attlee to the President, July 6, 1950. Harry S. Truman Library, Independence, MO.

———. Report of the United Nations Command Operations in Korea for the period 16-31 August 1950, transmitted by Ambassador Warren R. Austin, U.S. Representative to the United Nations, to the President of the Security Council, September 18, 1950. Harry S. Truman Library, Independence, MO.

———. The Conflict in Korea. *Far Eastern Series* 45, Pub. 4266. Washington, DC: Government Printing Office, 1951. Harry S. Truman Library, Independence, MO.

———. White House Press and Radio News Conference, President Harry S. Truman, June 29, 1950. Harry S. Truman Library, Independence, MO.

———. World Reaction to Korean Developments, No. 22, July 1950. Harry S. Truman Library, Independence, MO.

———. World Reaction to Korean Developments, Special Supplement, July 18, 1950. Harry S. Truman Library, Independence, MO.

———. World Reaction to Korean Developments, No. 27, July 24, 1950. Harry S. Truman Library, Independence, MO.

———. World Reaction to Korean Developments, No. 28, July 25, 1950. Harry S. Truman Library, Independence, MO.

———. World Reaction to Korean Developments, No. 29, July 26, 1950. Harry S. Truman Library, Independence, MO.

———. World Reaction to Korean Developments, No. 30, July 27, 1950. Harry S. Truman Library, Independence, MO.

———. World Reaction to President's Statement, No. 2, June 29, 1950. Harry S. Truman Library, Independence, MO.

U.S. National Security Council. A Report to the National Security Council by the Executive Security on United States Objectives and Programs for National Security, April 15, 1950. Harry S. Truman Library, Independence, MO.

Secondary Sources

Books

Arnold, James R. *Presidents Under Fire. Commanders in Chief in Victory and Defeat.* New York: Orion Books, 1994.

Astor, Gerald. *Presidents at War: From Truman to Bush, the Gathering of Military Power to Our Commanders in Chief.* Hoboken, NJ: Wiley & Sons, 2006.

Barclay, Glenn St John. *Friends in High Places: Australian-American Diplomatic Relations since 1945*. Melbourne: Oxford University Press, 1985.

Berridge, Geoffrey. "Britain, South African and African Defence, 1949-55." In *British Foreign Policy, 1945-56*, edited by Michael Dockrill and John W. Young, 101-25. New York: St. Martin's Press, 1989.

Blair, Clay. *The Forgotten War: America in Korea 1950-1953*. New York: Anchor Press, 1989.

Bullard, Sir Reader. *Britain and the Middle East: From Earliest Times to 1963*. London: Hutchinson University Library, 1964.

Craig, Gordon A. "The Political Leader as Strategist." In *Makers of Modern Strategy*, edited by Peter Paret, 481-509. New Jersey: Princeton University Press, 1986.

Cumings, Bruce. *The Origins of the Korean War. Liberation and the Emergence of Separate Regimes 1945-1947*. Princeton: Princeton University Press, 1981.

Delessert, Christian S. *Release and Repatriation of Prisoners of War at the End of Active Hostilities. A Study of Article 118, Paragraph 1 of the Third Geneva Convention Relative to the Treatment of Prisoners of War*. Zurich: Schulthess Polygraphischer Verlag, 1977.

Drew, S. Nelson. "Part I: Introduction. Paul Nitze and the Legacy of NSC-68." In *NSC-68: Forging the Strategy of Containment*, edited by S. Nelson Drew, 1-6. Washington, DC: National Defense University Press, 1996.

Dockrill, Michael. *British Defence since 1945*. Oxford, UK: Basil Blackwell, 1988.

Eayrs, James. *In Defence of Canada: Growing Up Allied*. Toronto: University of Toronto Press, 1980.

Farrar-Hockley, Anthony. *The British Part in the Korean War, Volume I: A Distant Obligation*. London: Her Majesty's Stationary Office, 1990.

Fehrenbach, T. R. *This Kind of War*. Dulles, VA: Potomac Books, 2008.

Fitzsimmons, M. A. *The Foreign Policy of the British Labour Government 1945-1951*. Notre Dame, IN: University of Notre Dame Press, 1953.

Foot, Rosemary. *A Substitute for Victory: The Politics of Peacemaking at the Korean Armistice Talks*. Ithaca, NY: Cornell University Press, 1990.

Freedman, Lawrence. "Introduction." In *British Foreign Policy, 1945-65*, edited by Michael Dockrill and John W. Young, 1-7. New York: St. Martin's Press, 1989.

Gaddis, John Lewis. *Strategies of Containment: A Critical Appraisal of Postwar American National Security Policy*. New York: Oxford University Press, 1982.

————. *We Now Know: Rethinking Cold War History*. New York: Oxford University Press, 1997.

Gallaway, Jack. *The Last Call of the Bugle: The Long Road to Kapyong*. Queensland: University of Queensland Press, 1999.

Gowing, Margaret. "Britain, America, and the Bomb." In *British Foreign Policy, 1945-65*, edited by Michael Dockrill and John W. Young, 31-46. New York: St. Martin's Press, 1989.

Grey, Jeffrey. *A Military History of Australia*. Melbourne: Cambridge University Press, 1999.

————. *The Commonwealth Armies and the Korean War*. Manchester, UK: Manchester University Press, 1988.

————. "The Regiment's First War: Korea, 1950-56." *In Duty First. A History of the Royal Australian Regiment*, 2nd ed., edited by David Horner and Jean Bou, 57-80. New South Wales: Allen & Unwin, 2008.

Hanson, Thomas E. *Combat Ready? The Eighth U.S. Army on the Eve of the Korean War*. College Station: Texas A&M University Press, 2010.

Hart, Stephen. *Montgomery and Colossal Cracks: the 21st Army Group in Northwest Europe, 1944-45*. Westport, CT: Praeger Publishing, 2000.

Herring, George C. *From Colony to Superpower: U.S. Foreign Relations since 1776*. New York: Oxford University Press, 2008.

House, Jonathan M. *A Military History of the Cold War, 1944-1962*. Norman: University of Oklahoma Press, 2012.

James, D. Clayton, with Anne Sharp Wells. *Refighting the Last War: Command and Crisis in Korea, 1950-1953*. New York: The Free Press, 1993.

Johnston, William. *A War of Patrols: Canadian Army Operations in Korea*. Vancouver: UBC Press, 2003.

Kaufman, Burton I. *The Korean War: Challenges in Crisis, Credibility, and Command*. Philadelphia: Temple University Press, 1986.

Kent, John. "Bevin's Imperialism and the Idea of Euro-Africa, 1945-49." In *British Foreign Policy, 1945-65*, edited by Michael Dockrill and John W. Young, 47-76. New York: St. Martin's Press, 1989.

Koldziej, Edward A. *The Uncommon Defense and Congress, 1945-1963*. Columbus: Ohio State University Press, 1966.

Lowe, Peter. *The Origins of the Korea War*. New York: Longman, 1986.

———. "The Significance of the Korean War in Anglo-American Relations, 1950-53." In *British Foreign Policy, 1945-56*, edited by Michael Dockrill and John W. Young, 126-148. New York: St. Martin's Press, 1989.

McCormack, Gavan. *Cold War, Hot War, An Australian Perspective on the Korean War*. Sydney: Hale and Iremonger, 1983.

Melady, John. *Korea: Canada's Forgotten War*. Toronto: MacMillan of Canada, 1983.

Moran, Lord. *Churchill: The Struggle for Survival 1945-60*. London: Sphere, 1968.

O'Neill, Robert. *Australia in the Korean War 1950-53. Volume I: Strategy and Diplomacy*. Canberra: Australian Government Publishing Service, 1981.

Odgers, George. *Across the Parallel: The Australian 77th Squadron with the United States Air Force in the Korean War*. Melbourne: William Heinemann, 1953.

Palazzo, Albert. *The Australian Army: A History of its Organisation*. Melbourne: Oxford University Press, 2001.

Pogue, Forrest C. *George C. Marshall: Statesman, 1945-1959*. New York: Viking, 1987.

Stairs, Denis. *The Diplomacy of Constraint: Canada, the Korean War, and the United States*. Toronto: University of Toronto Press, 1974.

Stebbins, Richard P. *The United States in World Affairs, 1950*. New York: Harper & Brothers, 1951.

Stubbs, Richard. "From Search and Destroy to Hearts and Minds: The Evolution of British Strategy in Malaya 1948-60." In *Counterinsurgency in Modern Warfare*. edited by Daniel Marston and Carter Malkasian, 101-18. Oxford: Osprey Publishing, 2010.

Trembath, Richard. *A Different Sort of War: Australians in Korea, 1950-53*. Melbourne: Australian Scholarly Publishing, 2005.

von Clausewitz, Carl. *On War*. Translated and Edited by Michael Howard and Peter Paret. Princeton: Princeton University Press, 1976.

Watson, Brent Byron. *Far Eastern Tour: The Canadian Infantry in Korea, 1950-1953*. Montreal: McGill-Queen's University Press, 2002.

Watt, Alan. *The Evolution of Australian Foreign Policy 1938-1965*. Cambridge: Cambridge University Press, 1967.

Weigley, Russell F. *The American Way of War: A History of United States Military Strategy and Policy*. Bloomington: Indiana University Press, 1973.

Wood, Herbert Fairlie. *Strange Battleground: Official History of the Canadian Army in Korea*. Ottawa: Queen's Printer, 1966.

Yockelson, Mitchell. *Borrowed Soldiers: Americans under British Command, 1918*. Norman: University of Oklahoma Press, 2008.

Periodicals

Albinski, Henry S. "Australia Faces China." *Asian Survey* 2, no. 2 (April 1962): 16-28.

Baldwin, Hanson W. "China as a Military Power." *Foreign Affairs* 30, no. 1 (October 1951): 51-62.

Blaxland, John C. "The Korean War: Reflections on Shared Australian and Canadian Military Experiences." *Canadian Military Journal* (Winter 2003-2004): 25-34.

Charmatz, Jan P., and Harold M. Wit. "Repatriation of Prisoners of War and the 1949 Geneva Convention." *The Yale Law Journal* 62, no. 3 (February 1953): 391-415.

Dingman, Roger. "Atomic Diplomacy during the Korean War." *International Security* 13, no. 3 (Winter 1988-1989): 50-91.

Dockrill, M. L. "The Foreign Office, Anglo-American Relations and the Korean War, June 1950-June 1951." *International Affairs (Royal Institute of International Affairs 1944)* 62, no. 3 (Summer 1986): 459-76.

Elliott, Mark. "The United States and Forced Repatriation of Soviet Citizens, 1944-47." *Political Science Quarterly* 88, no. 2 (June 1973): 253-75.

Gelber, Harry G. "Australia and the Great Powers." *Asian Survey* 15, no. 3 (March 1975): 187-201.

Grey, Jeffrey. "The Formation of the Commonwealth Division, 1950-1951." *Military Affairs* 51, no. 1 (January 1987): 12-16.

Halperin, Morton H. "The Limiting Process of the Korean War." *Political Science Quarterly* 78, no. 1 (March 1963): 13-39.

Harrod, Roy. "Hands and Fists Across the Sea." *Foreign Affairs* 30, no. 1 (October 1951): 63-76.

223

Holmes, John W. "Canada and the United States in World Politics." *Foreign Affairs* 40, no. 1 (October 1961): 105-17.

Jebb, Sir Gladwyn. "The Free World and the United Nations." *Foreign Affairs* 31, no. 3 (April 1953): 382-91.

Lowe, Peter. "An Ally and a Recalcitrant General: Great Britain, Douglas MacArthur and the Korean War, 1950-1." *The English Historical Review* 105, no. 416 (July 1990): 624-53.

McClellan, David S. "Dean Acheson and the Korean War." *Political Science Quarterly* 83, no. 1 (March 1968): 16-39.

Miles, Jr., Rufus E. "Hiroshima: The Strange Myth of Half a Million American Lives Saved." *International Security* 10, no. 2 (Autumn 1985): 121-40.

Millar, Thomas B. "Australia and the American Alliance." *Pacific Affairs* 37, no. 2 (Summer 1964): 148-60.

Millett, Allan R. "Introduction to the Korean War." *The Journal of Military History* 65, no. 4 (October 2001): 921-935.

Millis, Walter. "Military Problems of the New Administration." *Foreign Affairs* 31, no. 1 (January 1953): 215-24.

Peace Pledge Union. "Geneva Convention: An Introduction." http://www.ppu.org.uk/learn/texts/doc_geneva_con.html (accessed October 8, 2013).

Stairs, Denis. "Canada and the Korean War Fifty Years On." *Canadian Military History* 9, no. 3 (Summer 2000): 49-60.

Stevenson, Adlai. "Korea in Perspective." *Foreign Affairs* 30, no. 3 (April 1952): 349-60.

Stevenson, John A. "Canada, Free and Dependent." *Foreign Affairs* 29, no. 3 (April 1951): 456-67.

Swope, Kenneth. "Turning the Tide: The Strategic and Psychological Significance of the Liberation of Pyongyang in 1593." *War and Society* 21, no. 2 (October 2003): 1-22.

Tannenbaum, Frank. "The American Tradition in Foreign Relations." *Foreign Affairs* 30, no. 1 (October 1951): 31-50.

Government Documents

Bush, George W. "Address to a Joint Session of Congress and the American People, November 6, 2001." http://georgewbush-whitehouse.archives.gov/ news/releases/2001/09/20010920-8.html (accessed November 6, 2013).

Carney, Stephan A. CMH Pub 59-3-1, *Allied Participation in Operation Iraqi Freedom*. Washington, DC: Center of Military History, 2011. http://www.history.army.mil/ html/books/059/59-3-1/CMH_59-3-1.pdf (accessed November 7, 2013).

National Archives and Records Service. *Public Papers of the Presidents of the United States: Harry S. Truman, 1950*. Washington, DC: Government Printing Office, 1965.

Nichol, Jim. *Georgia [Republic]: Recent Developments and U.S. Interests*. Washington, DC: Congressional Research Service, 2012.

U.S. Department of Veterans Affairs. *Former American Prisoners of War (POWs)*. April, 2005. http://www.va.gov/vetdata/docs/SpecialReports/POWCY04Final4-7-05forweb.pdf (accessed November 8, 2013).

Monographs

Lai, David. "Learning from the Stones: A *GO* Approach to Mastering China's Strategic Concept, *Shi*." Monograph, U.S. Army War College, Strategic Studies Institute, Carlisle PA, 2004. http://www.strategicstudiesinstitute.army.mil/pubs/ display.cfm?pubID=378 (accessed October 15, 2013).

www.ingramcontent.com/pod-product-compliance
Lightning Source LLC
Chambersburg PA
CBHW081206280526
45787CB00006B/2351